AFTER COMPLETION

After Completion

The Later Letters of
Charles Olson and Frances Boldereff

EDITED BY SHARON THESEN AND RALPH MAUD

Talonbooks

Talonbooks
278 East First Avenue, Vancouver, British Columbia, Canada V5T 1A6
www.talonbooks.com

First printing: 2014

Typeset in Sabon
Printed and bound in Canada on 100% post-consumer recycled paper

Cover design by Lucy Wilner
Cover photograph of Charles Olson by Renate Gerhardt, courtesy Kate Olson Archive
Cover photograph of Frances Boldereff courtesy Lucy Wilner

Talonbooks gratefully acknowledges the financial support of the Canada Council for the Arts, the Government of Canada through the Canada Book Fund, and the Province of British Columbia through the British Columbia Arts Council and the Book Publishing Tax Credit.

Library and Archives Canada Cataloguing in Publication

Olson, Charles, 1910–1970 After completion : the later letters of Charles Olson and Frances Boldereff / Charles Olson and Frances Boldereff ; edited by Sharon Thesen and Ralph Maud.

Includes bibliographical references and index. ISBN 978-0-88922-706-4

1. Olson, Charles, 1910–1970—Correspondence. 2. Boldereff, Frances M. (Frances Motz), 1905– —Correspondence. 3. Olson, Charles, 1910–1970—Relations with women. 4. Poets, American—20th century—Correspondence. 5. Women critics—United States—Correspondence. I. Boldereff, Frances M. (Frances Motz), 1905– II. Thesen, Sharon, 1946– III. Maud, Ralph, 1928– IV. Title. V. Title: Later letters of Charles Olson and Frances Boldereff.

PS3529.L655Z48 2013 811'.54 C2013-901934-0

BEFORE COMPLETION
is the exhaustion of
the masculine.

AFTER COMPLETION
the finest clothes turn
to rags.

(Cheng Tzu gives another explanation.
He employs the image of a boat, and says,
"It has a leak, but there are rags for plugging it up.")

—*The I Ching or Book of Changes*
Bollingen Series XIX (1950), 712–14

CONTENTS

Introduction

SHARON THESEN

This edition of the correspondence between Charles Olson and Frances Boldereff continues from the point at which the earlier letters, collected in *A Modern Correspondence*, left off.[1] The present edition, *After Completion: The Later Letters*, begins at a transition in Olson and Boldereff's relationship, which, although always passionate and at times embattled, never returns for long to its previous level of fevered epistolary exchange. These letters present a more autonomous Boldereff and a more vulnerable Olson. They also reveal the modalities by which Boldereff and Olson continue their mutual project for Olson to "weave" Boldereff's words for her (no. 64, 20 November 1954) and for Boldereff to retain her role in Olson's life and imagination as muse, lover, and "Wise Goddess": the Salmon of Wisdom encoded in his poetry. Referred to as a "Circe" by Ralph Maud in *Charles Olson at the Harbor*,[2] Boldereff may very well have pulled Olson off course, but, in my view, to no transmogrifying effect. That she played a role in the destruction of Olson's relationship with Connie Olson and was a cause of stress in his relationship with Betty Olson cannot be denied: here is where Boldereff could also be judged a Siren. Whether Muse, Wise Goddess, Siren, or Circe, Frances Boldereff clearly belongs with powerful feminine archetypes. Her dynamism and what she referred to as her "fiery nature," her energetic critique of the "depraved sex morality" and "deadness" of American postwar culture, her aesthetic vision and her charm, were a touchstone for Olson for more than two decades. There was no one else like Boldereff in Olson's life, certainly no woman he loved as much and for so long.

1 Charles Olson and Frances Boldereff, ed. Ralph Maud and Sharon Thesen, *Charles Olson and Frances Boldereff: A Modern Correspondence* (Middletown, CT: Wesleyan University Press, 1999). Abbreviated hereafter *AMC*.

2 Ralph Maud, *Charles Olson at the Harbor* (Vancouver: Talonbooks, 2008), p. 51.

Charles Olson, 1949

Kate Olson Archive

Frances Boldereff, early 1940s

courtesy Lucy Wilner

After Completion: The Later Letters is a story of a "completed" love affair that continued to compel both Olson and Boldereff until Olson's death in 1970. That their letters would dwindle in number and intensity after 1950 seems an inevitability given their life circumstances.

"I am burned, abt words," Olson writes to Boldereff. "They did you damage. They ran ahead, of acts" (no. 2, 18 September 1950). Two weeks earlier, Boldereff, increasingly frustrated after Olson's promising and then failing to visit her in Brooklyn, had informed him about an affair she had begun with a young man she had met on the subway (no. 324, 3 September 1950, *AMC*). Olson's being "burned, abt words" could indicate that his own words in his letters (in which he was promising to visit her) were ultimately damaging to Boldereff. Or, perhaps the "words" Olson is referring to are Boldereff's, indicating a recklessness (i.e., her telling Olson about the affair) that had damaging consequences by "burning" him. Olson's tone suggests a betrayal has occurred which is worse than Boldereff's apparent infidelity; for, as he goes on to say, "this is evil, where it is not art." Olson and Boldereff had recently been reiterating the terms of their much-discussed bargain, that his "words" (not only his letters but his works, which Boldereff believed also spoke for her) were his "acts" of love toward her. Olson seems convinced, although he does not say so explicitly, that this alchemy (words being acts, and, specifically, his words being his acts) would pertain in his relationship with Boldereff regardless of the dilemma posed by his common-law marriage to Connie Olson. The terms of their relationship, however, included Boldereff's language and ideas being "woven" by Olson into literary form, so that the words that were Olson's acts also belonged to her and to some degree originated in her. But the delicate balance of this circulation of words and acts is about to topple.

Revolt is brewing in Boldereff's letters. She is cruelly critical of Olson's relationship with Edward Dahlberg, tying Dahlberg to her disgusted opinion of the "life-denying" forces in American culture[3]—a view that Olson, on eggshells at this point, reluctantly accepts (no. 321, 1 September 1950, *AMC*). Boldereff tells Olson how frustrated she is both by his broken

3 Olson's friendship with Edward Dahlberg in the fraught late-summer months of 1950 provoked an outburst from Boldereff, with whom Olson had been parsing the difficulties of his relationship with this fellow poet. She writes, "the lines you quote me out of him are absolute filth" and adds, "I have been examining this kind of thing in the Hebrew for twenty some years—it is where I am their declared open enemy—and I have a sword in my hand to turn against all who defame or cheapen life" (no. 316, 30 August 1950, *AMC*). Believing herself to be competing with Dahlberg for Olson's unreliable attention at that time, her animosity was dramatically exaggerated. Nevertheless, an opposition to "semitic" cultural forms occasionally recurs in Boldereff's letters until the mid-1950s.

promises and her own failure to get and keep a job in the publishing industry.[4] "When Olson will you arrive?" she asks at the end of a letter in which she has declared that Arthur Rimbaud "belongs" to her, that he "was the poet—I the words" (no. 317, 30 August 1950, *AMC*). On 3 September 1950, in the letter in which Boldereff informs Olson about the young African-American man she met on the subway, she copies out Louise Varèse's translation of Rimbaud's "Morning of Drunkenness" (the one that famously ends "The time of the Assassins is here"), telling Olson that every word of the poem was directed toward him. Olson, in the meantime, was in Washington, D.C., too ill with the flu even to go down to the mailbox where Boldereff's letter was waiting. The shocked words that begin this volume of the correspondence are Olson's: "Am still stunned, astonied," he writes, "stunned, astonied, 'pended" (no. 1, 12 September 1950).

The letters from August 1950 until the crisis of the Labor Day weekend distill the tensions in the Olson-Boldereff dynamic and herald new dynamics to come. After the "completion" of the passionate momentum of their correspondence by Boldereff's fling, which at least served to gain Olson's renewed attention, these later letters reflect a further separation of their energies and preoccupations: Olson's into the composition of the *Maximus* poems and the demands of his career as a leading poet, theorist, and teacher; and Boldereff's into her work as a print designer, author, exegete, and "lover of man-created beauty," especially in the form of Rimbaud's poetry (no. 324, 3 September 1950, *AMC*). We see Rimbaud's poetry becoming Boldereff's touchstone as Olson works more and more experimentally in the later essays and *Maximus* poems, articulating a world view in which Boldereff was less and less implicated. While Olson and Boldereff's correspondence had the effect of emboldening and encouraging them both, most of the emboldening and encouraging went in Olson's direction. In a letter near the beginning of this volume, Olson rues "words running ahead of acts" but reiterates his commitment to their mutual comprehension of "where the beauty lies, the real business—what you and I at least must raise ... what we are here on earth for" (no. 2, 18 September 1950).

Although Boldereff's letters from September 1950 to May 1952 are missing, we can extrapolate from Olson's replies that Boldereff has been laying down conditions and, at times, threatening to stop writing altogether. But

4 Boldereff writes to Olson that she had "the honor to be fired once more—my 165th time!" (no. 113, 1 November 1967). She describes quarrels with employers about their poor printing standards and confusing jargon. Boldereff's working life in the printing business was long and varied. She managed all the print production for Pennsylvania State College in the late 1940s and worked in the production departments at various New York publishing houses in the Brooklyn years—in addition to designing and supervising the private printing of her own books on James Joyce.

as much as he appreciates the references, annotations, and observations her letters provide, Olson values the great vivacity of Boldereff herself. Even when Boldereff accuses Olson of "feeding off" her, Olson's reply is, "well, what, frances motz, should, by yr own wisdom, be more wonderful? what?" (no. 9, 13 November 1950). As Olson's "sweet salmon," and within their mutual high estimation of the resuscitating qualities of her lovemaking, Boldereff is hardly in a position to disagree. A letter from her, he says, "still causes me to lift, and ride, and go places i am not otherwise taken," but that more than a letter is "the image of you ... which could not possibly cease to live in me, no matter what" (no. 6, 14 October 1950). Even so, when it is apparent Boldereff suggests they have a "closer" relationship, Olson demurs, for "moving it forward ... into closerness" would endanger "the depth & power of letters between us, the imaginative wildness of the communication, would be disturbed" (no. 6, 14 October 1950). Fearing the consequences of a domestication of his relationship with Boldereff, Olson is also trying to protect his marriage—at this point to Connie Olson and then, later, to Betty Olson—from his attachment to Boldereff. The possibility that they might live together was broached and rejected later on, by each of them in different ways and under different circumstances.

The correspondence ceases altogether while Olson and Connie spend February through June 1951 in the Yucatán, after which time and "weeping, to leave,"[5] Olson returns to Black Mountain College in North Carolina. There is no record of exchange between Olson and Boldereff until he visits her in Brooklyn in April 1952. Perhaps by visiting Boldereff again, after a hiatus in the correspondence that may have allowed them to let their love affair subside without the drama of official separation, he hopes to recapture some of the physical happiness he had experienced in the Yucatán: "sex is the sun of the body ... there would be no life in its absence" (no. 14, 21 April 1952). He writes to Boldereff after their reunion, "it is by your life that I feel embraced. This, surely, is union" (no. 14). Subsequent visits until November 1952 precipitate Connie's decision to leave Olson, a separation made permanent after Olson begins an affair with Betty Kaiser, a music student at Black Mountain College who becomes pregnant with Olson's child. After the dissolution of Black Mountain College in 1957, the new family (Olson, his common-law wife, Betty, and their son, Charles Peter) settle in Gloucester, Massachusetts. There, in the house at 28 Fort Square with windows looking out to the sea, Olson can write for long, late hours and entertain visitors and acolytes on his own terms.

5 Tom Clark, *Charles Olson: The Allegory of a Poet's Life* (New York: Norton, 1991), p. 202.

Charles Olson had by 1950 been engaged in extensive correspondence with Robert Creeley, as well as researching, writing, and, through teaching and conversation, articulating the projectivist poetics that made him one of the most important and influential poets and theorists to emerge from the early postmodernist New American Poetry scene. Frances Boldereff was an outsider to this scene and its discourse, a single mother and book designer with no secure employment in the notoriously sexist publishing industry of New York in the 1950s and '60s. During this period, she worked in the production departments of several New York publishing houses, including Van Nostrand and Doubleday. She was also writing and publishing, via her own Classic Non-Fiction Library imprint, exegeses of James Joyce's *Finnegans Wake*, beginning with *Reading Finnegans Wake* in 1959. It was as "designer" that Boldereff first introduced herself to Olson when she wrote to him in praise of *Call Me Ishmael* (no. 1, 22 November 1947, *AMC*); and as "designer," "compiler," "guide," and "reader" that she impoverished herself putting forward her research on increasingly esoteric sources in *Finnegans Wake* and *Ulysses*. Publishing her own books to her own exacting standards and at tremendous expense is for Boldereff not negotiable;[6] neither is the expense associated with sending her daughter, Lucinda, to good schools.

Financial problems drag at Olson as well in the earlier years that comprise the letters in this volume. Olson tells Boldereff about his efforts, as rector, to keep Black Mountain College's finances afloat. Reduced to selling off landholdings and cattle, composing fundraising letters to potential donors, dealing with peripatetic faculty, staff, and students, Olson is consumed by the "24 hour miseries of trying to keep a little polis alive in the monstrous bland quantitative present" (no. 72, 22 February 1956). Even so, Black Mountain College provides institutional space for Olson's performative pedagogy. In the same letter quoted above, Olson tells Boldereff he "caught fire and went 7 hours, and so much I sd ... sounded as much yrs as mine. In fact yrs ...

6 *Hermes to His Son Thoth: Being Joyce's Use of Giordano Bruno in Finnegans Wake* (1967) cost $4,800 to print—savings of $19,000 on a $24,000 estimate. Boldereff had given her printer $1,000 as a down payment, not knowing she was to lose her job at Van Nostrand the next day. See Boldereff's letter of 6 November 1967 (no. 117), in which she mentions the typesetting labour of "a young negro" whom the printer had "found" in one of the "schools of Trenton." The back flap of the book is devoted to two of the three typesetters who worked on this complicated text—not to Boldereff herself as author, or even the book's subject, Giordano Bruno. Here, Boldereff writes about "the heroic role" played by the "manufacturers" of the book: Edward A. Krupa Jr. and Stanley J. Kuliczkowski. "It was a costly and difficult manuscript to set because in order to make crystal clear to the reader five sets of writing, five styles of typesetting had to be evolved." Boldereff likens the typesetters' achievement to that of Drake and Hawkins who "regarded Queen Elizabeth's niggardliness as a stimulus to performance."

sounds more right than my own mouthings and firings." His position at the college also allows him to create radical curricula and affords him opportunities to invite friends, associates, and admired others to teach and do research. But Boldereff begins to express concern about Olson's life at Black Mountain. Despite her admiration for the "handsome" first issue of *Black Mountain Review*, by early 1955 she tells Olson that she is "very unhappy about your magazine [*Black Mountain Review*], your writing, your relation to life, in fact everything ... if you go on in your present ways you are done for" (no. 69, 27 January 1955). At Black Mountain, Boldereff assumes, Olson is "alone in a very dangerous way," receiving "no criticism and no stimulation" (no. 76, 5 November 1956). In the same letter, she criticizes the newly published *Maximus Poems 11–22* for lacking "the same force and weight as in the others." *Call Me Ishmael* is the work of Olson's Boldereff consistently champions, going so far as to try to have it reprinted as a Doubleday Anchor book while she is employed at the Doubleday office in New York. It is the work that most effectively addresses, according to Boldereff, the problem of "America," which for Boldereff is coincident with the condition of "woman": problems that Boldereff would eventually consider adequately addressed (and even solved) in the poetry of Arthur Rimbaud. Even James Joyce, whose work she studied deeply for many decades, failed to rise to the occasion of her intellectual and feminist standards, with his disappointing search for the "'eternal' feminine," which made Boldereff feel "ill all over" (no. 75, 11 September 1956).

As observers and readers of this correspondence, we should not be too terribly shocked, given Boldereff's various expressions of disappointment in the course of Olson's career and private life, that she should announce in the fall of 1964 that she has met "someone more truly Maximus" than Olson and is planning to move in with him (no. 97, 9 September 1964). Provoked to outrage, and in a long, emphatic cry of protest, Olson lays out what he sees as Boldereff's most damaging and self-damaging (although in many ways productive) practice of electing male writers to ventriloquize her feminist and vitalist life philosophy. Olson rebukes Boldereff for using men's "lives words work or beliefs as *though they were yours*." Alluding to Boldereff's frequent assertions that she herself was "not a writer" and to his having assumed the mantle of singular poet-hero ("Maximus") to Boldereff's muse function, Olson admonishes Boldereff's habit of using male writers and artists as literary proxies: "you ... have no confidence in your use of language: but you don't *leave* it there. You take *men's* use of language" (no. 98, 12 September 1964). For years, Olson had been encouraging Boldereff to articulate her own thoughts in her own words: "make it wholly your own speech, leaving out all these literary characters!" he writes. "It is my old cry, that, if you say this much, you *must* say more—spell it out" (no. 52, 20 March 1954).

Having already declared early on that Rimbaud "was the poet—[she] the words" (no. 317, 30 August 1950, *AMC*), and after reading Rimbaud so closely that she believes that "it is as though [she is] literally Rimbaud in female form" (no. 39, 4 July 1953), Boldereff seems no longer to be holding Olson to the pact they had agreed to: Boldereff's "obedience" to Olson's genius and autonomy would yield results, emotional and intellectual, that reflected her vitalist life philosophy. There is also the matter of their physical separation that by this time, and given Olson's remarriage, has become status quo. If Boldereff's dedication to Rimbaud supplanted her dedication to Olson, it is understandable that by redirecting her hopes and beliefs toward a vision already articulated by Rimbaud, she constructs a less-problematic collaboration with a powerful male poet.

Olson co-operates with this defection to the extent of suggesting, in the summer of 1954, that Boldereff write a translation and gloss of Rimbaud's "Credo in Unam." The resulting text, which she refers to as her only "literary poem," is her "attempt to define ... the task of modern woman" (no. 59, 2 August 1954). The task of modern woman, as Boldereff discerns it through Rimbaud's poetry, is to return to the gendered gestures that compose an archaic world view. "Like Rimbaud," Boldereff writes in her gloss on the text, "I am enamoured of woman at the time of the Minoans." She includes a lengthy transcribed excerpt from Arthur Evans's *The Palace of Minos*, overlaying the text with tissue reproductions of Minoan art. Rimbaud's "credo," achieved in the feminine register ("unam" rather than "unum"), is in Boldereff's translation, "I believe in wholeness" (no. 59, 2 August 1954). Olson's poem "I Believe in You" is his reply (no. 60, 9 August 1954).

Boldereff's idiosyncratic, utopian-archaic feminism anticipates French feminism's *jouissance* as the feminine knowledge and authority Boldereff endeavoured to recover in the imagination of Arthur Rimbaud. Joy, not possession, was the ideal Boldereff aspired to as a woman, as a scholar, as Olson's muse and mistress, interlocutor and reader—and to knowledge itself. Her study of Joyce, Blake, and Rimbaud supplied the authority of history, myth, vitalist élan, and gnostic philosophy for whatever in her was irrepressible and "fiery"—qualities she admits may have "ruined" her "success in life" (no. 132, 4 February 1968).

This volume of the later letters of Charles Olson and Frances Boldereff completes the trajectory of a dynamic, creative relationship that demonstrably inflected Olson's thought. It was only with the publication of Tom Clark's biography of Olson that Frances Boldereff's existence in Olson's life, let alone her importance to him, were publicized. From an understandable desire to maintain discretion or to avoid damaging consequences, Olson had veiled Boldereff's existence from public view. Perhaps he was dismayed by her intolerances and exactingness. Toward Boldereff personally, that is, in his letters, he is respectful, tender, generous, and loving. It could not have been easy for Olson, at the times when he was most vulnerable, to realize that in Boldereff he had had a true companion. Unsent—and some sent—letters in this volume express regret and confusion. Even though Olson's childhood Catholicism would have contributed to his lifelong insistence on "words as acts," suggesting the imprint of the transubstantive "word made flesh" of the Eucharist in his literary and erotic practices, this formula must at times have been a bitter pill for Boldereff to swallow. In conversation with me in 1994, Boldereff said that Olson's "was a very heavy demand. I wasn't getting anything back as a woman: *What the hell does she want? I'm writing to her.*"[7]

The by now much decried masculinism, sexism, and racism of Cold War America also would have underwritten the terms of their relationship. The near-parodic masculinism of Olson's 1950 "Projective Verse" manifesto can be seen as encouraged by Boldereff's permissively phallic outlook. She writes in March 1950 about the "deep parallel between my Blake and your Melville ... and I now am sure that out of this worthless mess we have here we must somehow bring what they asked of us. And I believe the coming engine with its steam up is desirable—let the whole rottenness fall" (no. 158, 10 March 1950, *AMC*) so as to make the new, necessary "open ground" which would remove "the sting" of relations between the sexes: "All men and women have been dreaming for 10 000 years of the day when the sexes shall be no more—but for myself I have struggled to find that way that *with* the very present sex we now have to remove the thorn of it ... So my answer to you about you—about the poet—*has* to be what you do, what you are—10 000 years—10 000" (no. 159, 11 March 1950, *AMC*). Obviously, "Projective Verse" was not Olson's final word but among the first in a series of iterations. Olson was "after" something in poetry that he believed had been either hidden or taken from it; he sought to recover it "among stones," as he writes in his 1949 poem "The Kingfishers." Early on, Boldereff had keyed him in with her phrase "humanism and its errors" (no. 264, 26 July 1950, *AMC*).

There is a similarity, I think, between Frances Boldereff and George Eliot's conception of the character of Dorothea in the novel *Middlemarch*. There, in the "Finale," the reader is encouraged to agree that although Dorothea, like her avatar Saint Theresa, was "foundress of nothing," "the effect of her being on those around her was incalculably diffusive." If we agree, as I suggest the correspondence invites us to, that Boldereff's life, hopes, energies, and

7 Frances Boldereff, in conversation with Sharon Thesen, Woodward, PA, summer 1994.

words are inscribed in Olson's work, the effect of "her being" on twentieth-century poetry and poetics is "incalculably diffusive."

The entire correspondence could be seen as a Rimbaldian study of poetic imagination, "the magical study / which happiness is," as Olson writes in his 1956 Rimbaud-influenced poem "Variations Done for Gerald Van De Wiele." From the beginning of the correspondence in 1947, Boldereff charges Olson with the task of alerting America to its materialist torpor, its Blakean "Sleep of Ulro." When I asked her in 1994 about her hopes for America, she said, "I guess it depends on how goddamn unhappy do we get before we start to wake up." Boldereff was still sharply critical of American culture, and the project she initially charged Olson with, to awaken America, still preoccupied her, and was still alive in her own investigations into the archaic sources of William Blake, Arthur Rimbaud, and James Joyce.

A NOTE ON THE TEXT

We have taken it as our responsibility to correct silently many of the correspondence's misspellings and unintentional punctuation lapses. However, to preserve the vitality of these personal communications, inconsistencies in spelling and capitalization have been allowed to stand. In Olson's letters especially, idiosyncrasies have been retained when they were judged to be deliberate. For example, he sometimes opened a parenthesis without closing it or hyphenated words in unexpected and unconventional ways.

The paragraphing and spacing of the original typed and handwritten letters have been approximated insofar as the constraints of a printed volume will allow. Underlined text in the original letters has been set in italics. Note that the occasional "(?)" is Olson's not the editors', as are the ellipses (...). Square brackets are used for any editorial intrusion.

As an aid to understanding oblique references in the letters, readers may refer to abbreviations and full names of people and places in the annotated index.

Letter no. 77 (31 May 1957) and letter no. 102 (20 March 1965) are in the possession of Lucy Wilner. All other letters reproduced in this volume are held in the Charles Olson Research Collection, Archives and Special Collections at the Thomas J. Dodd Research Center, University of Connecticut Libraries, Storrs, Connecticut (abbreviated "Storrs"). Letters from Boldereff to Olson are contained in boxes 130–131; letters from Olson to Boldereff are contained in boxes 183–185.

The Later Letters

Part One

12 SEPTEMBER 1950–18 DECEMBER 1950

"There came to me straight out of God's hand a beautiful young negro" (no. 324, 3 September 1950, *AMC*). With these words Frances Boldereff shattered any dream Charles Olson might have had that he could hold on to her by letters alone. He took the train from Washington, D.C., to New York to assess the damage, and continued on to his mother's house in Gloucester, Massachusetts. It is from there he writes the forlorn first letter of this volume, recognizing that the romantic side of the relationship has spent itself.

After this completion, what is left? The second letter (written when Olson was safely back with his wife, Connie, in Washington) sets the sights afresh: the "real business" with Boldereff is to persist in finding out "where the beauty lies" (no. 2, 18 September 1950). And the long letter drawing on D.H. Lawrence (no. 5, 5 October 1950) points toward the beauty of laws "on which to erect new civilization." Clearly Boldereff still inspires, but without her letters from this period, we do not know exactly how. When she invites Olson for a visit, he backs off again (no. 11, 5 December 1950).

This phase of attempted rediscovery ends, with some relief, when Olson finds himself able to draw $200 from his retirement fund and make a long-awaited trip with Connie to Mexico.

RM

1

Gloucester to Brooklyn[1]
12 September 1950 (postmark)

tuesday

frances:

Am still stunned, astonied. This is only to touch you, to tell you I am merely so bewildered I do not know what to say. Nor do I mean you stunned me. I stunned myself, I think it better be put.

Please write me if you are all right, how the job situation is, and how Etcetera is. I shall be here a few more days before making trip to see friend Creeley.[2]

stunned, astonied, 'pended

charles

1 Boldereff's address is 5 Monroe Place, Brooklyn 2, New York. The return address on the envelope is "Stage Fort Avenue, Gloucester, Massachusetts." Olson was visiting his mother.

2 On 16 September 1950, Olson sent Robert Creeley a telegram saying that he had to return immediately to Washington and could not visit him.

2

Washington to Brooklyn
18 September 1950 (postmark 18 September 1950)

Monday Sept 18

Frances:

This was to have been written to you from Gloucester. But in the push yesterday …

And do not mind, please, that I don't write just for the moment. I have to break the pattern. I am burned, abt words. They did you damage. They ran ahead, of acts. This is evil, where it is not art. I am merely simplifying, & clearing—as we sd, to get back to the conditions of *Ishmael* or *Trinacria*.

And the Irish & the Swede, so far as the man goes. *BUT*, do not you forget what I sd last, abt where the beauty lies, the real business—what you and I at least must raise, can, do have the sights for,—what we are here on earth for.

Love

Charles

3

Washington to Brooklyn (special delivery)
22 September 1950 (postmark)

friday

frances—

Still picking way forward but by God you shall have at least this note, the bad businesses you write about[3] angering me ((next time, next job, make them let you go to work on the spot (don't trust 'em—they get scared of you)—or get a contract from these people who *promise* jobs, or mss.))

And continue to take care of yourself—your health, as well as yr eyes—right now, frances, right now especially

Love,
Charles

3 This letter, along with any others Boldereff may have written until 4 May 1952, is missing.

4

Washington to Brooklyn
29 September 1950 (postmark 29 September 1950)

friday

frances—

Will write you, decently, tomorrow (d.v)

been ill, with evil, fluctuant flu

but all's well—that is, do work (throw self there: what else?)

the damages

love

O

5

Washington to Brooklyn
5 October 1950 (postmark 5 October 1950)

thurs 10/5/50

frances:

the trouble is, how to say anything, so much was sd that was crazy (i mean, over here, this guy) how to write (almost like how it was, to begin with, not abc's, but later, when, to put words down, and make them behave (what do i know, abt that? fact is, that's all i know)

so you musn't mind. it's me that's confused, not really but yes, puzzled, to put ahead communication with you. you see, frances, you got to be a huge part of my concentration. and to break that kind of concentration off, to get a clearing, is why i am so damn stupidly silent. (we know, how dangerous it is, for this character, the way he follows language in, instead of, vice versa, don't we?)

but, at the same time, i wouldn't (you may, of course) be so sure abt affection & love viz ol-son (pronounced egu) i am presented with this query: (for you know how it is—one does have to go by what one is, there is no other way) anyhow, if, as you say, i know where we are, then i am sure that whitman's notions of affection & love are out of business, that i am much more sure that lawrence is right, in kangaroo, (more importantly even than in his job on whitman himself) that, these words, that whole notion, the adhesive, is rotted from head to foot, that there is direct connection between UN or Communism & the intimate, on goals & ends as previously formulated, that, if we are to move, these words too—like life, & soul—have to be renewed. And words are only renewed by what they represent, itself, being renewed.

I wld take it one step further than "Somers"—the step, i take it, DHL himself took it, in Escaped Cock, part I (only): that the thing is, to hear, ultimately, as it is, the clang of a cock; and that such hearing, to find the secret of it, is, worth coming back, putting behind one, overlooking, a Cruxifiction.[4]

I think where even he went off (Part II) is, abandoning the possibility even Somers is faced with, (comes to): that we are, essentially, guerrillas, partisans, frontier creatures, maquis, even here, where the old essentials are, where, they took root. And that the mark of new man & woman, is, that fraught question, why, am I never lonely, have i ever been, lonely?

(My guess is, that, it is because we have been *forced* to triangulate *two* realities: the human, which is, is it not, actually only a stop to consolidate gains which are actually made, not by human reality but by that larger reality which we dub nature. And that this position of mediatorship, that we are now in, is—from the old gauges—does look like, from that old vantage—"cold, inhuman, unlivered, non-visceral" or whatever I have been recently charged with being, from another source.

It can be put another way: that it is not a question of a loss or lack of love & affections, but of the way they are expressed, that, confronted as we are by rot and the will to undo, to go ahead, we characters dispose ourselves as much a-slant and cocked here as we have to towards external reality (which is moving so fast, and curiously, before us: treacherously, too). Why shld we crack a twig, here, any more than there?

Which is why, when you cry, the barbaric ignorance of the Americans, I say, pooh, it's true, but when you've sd it, what have you sd, where are you? To hell with the Americans. Look at yrself—or, my classic answer, curious, that these barbarians, have thrown up poets and scholars (as well as engineers) to dominate the earth's work, in our time.

Generalization, now, is as dead as peace is, as war, is. There is one requirement only (and it, curiously enough, carries in it, does it not, one of the very clues on which love (the concept of) exists. That requirement is, stay OPEN, at all costs, stay OPEN, in order to be IN.

It's gone far beyond survival, personal survival or any kind. It is not negative, or is it any longer useful to take either anarchistic position (generally the Bohemian) or the nihilistic (generally, the intellectual, I mean the fine, high mind).

It is become a question, like this: these are the *bases* on which to erect new civilization, these very

4 Olson seems to be deliberately playing with words here, as he does in his subsequent essay "The Escaped Cock."

apparent contradictions. (The truth is, all they contradict, is, what was, what we have known, *not* human possibility, which, as I think, is to be circumscribed *only* by that other reality, which includes the human.

You know, frances, we are, all of us, so goddamn glib, abt what is human. We really ought to open our eyes. The funny thing is, was there ever a time, when, with the eyes open, there were so many new things to be seen—new men (horrible, surely, some of them yes, but—fr the eye of nature—well ... And, by her laws, fr horror or shapelessness ...

I honestly don't know.

But I am doomed to speculate. My function is, simply, to do what presents itself to me. I am the only answer god gives me. I take it, now, we all have to be, in a way (and it is not comfortable) simply because the situation is OPEN. It may have been blown open, sure. But it is open. And that's what we have, to work with.

Write me again, and, recognize,

this is love,

charles

o yes, (1) the Fr printer is,
Maaster Lescaret
3 Rue Cardinale
(The Black Sun Press)
Paris

& i shall do what you ask, abt Kaggli, but,
that little bastard, he hasn't answered me in
l yr and a half (& the last letter was to get fr him a drawing of my puss or head for the coming mag-book, which he ignored)

6

Washington to Brooklyn
14 October 1950 (postmark 14 October 1950)

saturday 10/14/50

frances:

the point is, you do call me out, will, i am sure, just as long as i live. now the devil is, that i am a writer. as you surely more than anyone comprehend, that means that to write is the fullest expression, can be (almost always is) an excluding thing, the main track on which one runs. after all, it was a letter of yours which brought us together (the book, that cold bizness which writing produces, sitting out there, not so much a cause as your own capacity to take yr response and throw it out, project it, into the known: a book goes, willy-nilly (even a letter on this cold side of the moon of a letter), into the *un*known.

i say this, simply because, that you say, let this correspondence cease if it does not stick to yr conditions ... Frances, if the bizness no longer does give you the return it did, i am telling you it does, me (curious thing is, that letter i wrote you last week did what you have always invoked, and i shall toss in copy, with this, to show you.[5] it is what i mean, how, no matter what, you do lead me on—one example.)

the trouble is, when, as you now do, you feel i have acted badly ("small" is yr word), it puts terrible restraints on things, whole areas of things one does not speak of, i suppose (i feel it myself, even to sending you the enclosed, it seems so god damn "literary" a thing to do, such a "literary" use of feeling. what i mean is, i don't feel that myself, but, the thought that you might—damn well may—(and, for cause, i can recognize), is hindering (i certainly shall never forget that last—almost last—remark of yrs, quoting quitman, that all you get, is letters!)

5 Olson enclosed a draft of his piece on D.H. Lawrence's *The Man Who Died*, published as "The Escaped Cock" in *Origin* 2 (Summer 1951) and in *Human Universe*.

that is, straight, obviously, the truth. now, for reasons aforesaid, (& afore!), that seems to me more than a fact: it becomes (has been, is,—as I say—will be) a very important fact, to me one of the most important (you will remember how, from my very first moves to see you, how gingerly i was, for fear that, moving it forward—as, inevitably, i dare say, it had to—into closerness, this very thing—the depth & power of letters between us, the imaginative wildness of the communication, would be disturbed

crazy thing is (really, such facts are so beautiful, frances) no such thing has happened, olson-wise. i feel even closer, even deeper. but that, fr yr point of view, i was "small", that's blighting, has to be fought, even by me. And i can see how it may well be (for you) the straw to bring the whole house down. I pray not. I cannot, of course, do what you say: leave out bahs. We must—to keep anything alive—not cut corners, keep things open. And hell, frances: what use wld i be to you if i were not—here, at least, where i excuse my very existence—"muscular," sometimes, as you disastrously & accurately put it! (That sharp critique, is, registered, in my mind, like that other, back there, which i can never remember the precise phrasing of (a purposeful forgetting of the organism, i am sure, you were so way down inside the machinery of my own process; no one, ever, put it, that close)

do what you can, frances. And don't have it a burden (you have enough to carry). For the truth is (the answer to why a letter still causes me to lift, and ride, and go places i am not otherwise taken) is, that, more important than a letter, is, the image of you, which comes from the beginning (before, even!) & which could not possibly cease to live in me, no matter what. Love, C

[encl. carbon copy of "The Escaped Cock" typescript]

The Escaped Cock: Notes on Lawrence & the Present, or, the Real

1.

I take it that CONTEST is what puts drama (what they keep harping on still as story, plot) into the thing: the writer's contesting with reality—to see it, to SEE; that climax is not what happens to the characters or things (which is, even at the finest, a rigged puppet-demonstrandum) but is, instead, what another, my peer, called "a broken stump," this contest, and its issue, the ISSUE of, the man who writes. The issue is what causes CHANGE (the struggle inside, the contest there, inside, *exhibited*). At root (or stump) what *is*, is no longer THINGS but WHAT HAPPENS *BETWEEN* THINGS, these are the terms of the reality contemporary to us—

and the terms of what we are. If form is no more than an extension of content, then the proposition reads thus: content (contest leading to issue arriving at change equals) form.

Myself, I take it, DHL explored the problem, was, at end, so attacking.

(1) ETRUSCAN PLACES—terminus of that extraordinary contest, Lawrence vs place, ideal place, end to the going-round-the-earth-to find it, finding it there, Civitavecchia. And the work of the last fifty months of his life, following, thereon.

(2) LADY CHATTERLEY'S LOVER: the act of simplification to get objects in to exert *other than psychological or introspective effects*, by the pulling out of the cloth ONE (red, Guatemala red, Pompeian red, for that matter, Etruscan or Sumerian RED) THREAD; and that the simplest if sturdiest of all, sex, and itself, here, the physical or animal, straight, here, and (only here excusable) the word orgasm as issue intended, that is, the triumph or delight of same as Mellors is capable of its teaching.

This—the act of simplification, the same to be carefully seen as utterly different from the *elementary* (even Stein)—he also does in (3) THE ESCAPED COCK, Part I. It is not so easy to put the simplification this time except that it is a direct question, the question the Man Who Died asks himself, on his return: is anything worth more than the most precise sharpening of the instrument, a human, to the hearing of—the hearing of *all* there *is in*— the bronze clang of a cock's crow? (Is an X-fiction worth a cock's crow?)

In other words the next step down from Lady Chatterley's L was to the dark or phallic god who is not phallic or penissimus alone but the dark as night the forever dark, the going-on of you-me-whoever as conduit of that dark, the well-spring, whatever it is. The next step down (out of the light, into the painted tomb, back into the shell, the painted shell, goes) THE ESCAPED COCK, is THE WHOLE SENSES as simplified from (as the next step to) the FIRST SENSE, sex. (Part 2 fails miserably, apparently because, at this new stage of narrative Lawrence was not yet able to take woman down that next step towards his etruria. His "woman" here loses by goddessissing the actuality of Constance (Frieda), an actuality the Christ gains. (Always the man leads Lawrence, in?)

2.

beauty, sd the Bearded Man
in inception, in continuation, and in end

The thing is—has got so (love, affection, friendship: the dying into, or whatever)—has already become the FACT, is now more than, is what DHL projected in EC Part 1, is, viz:

that the thing, that what happens between, is: to hear, absolute, as it is, the SOUND, that crow ("gold," he sd, the Man) or (as another) of another his chicken fine bird he is, two ends like they say, clean straight barring Jimmy (his father, also Jimmy, the same);

and that such hearing (to find the secret of it, which means, of course, to recognize it, then to admit it, then, of all, to participate) is worth the coming back, the putting behind one, the over-looking, a Crucifixtion.

It strikes me that where even DHL went off (Part 2) was the abandoning of that possibility which even Somers (kangaroo) and Mellors came to admit: that we are, all of us, now, essentially guerrillas—maquis, frontier or side-street—EVEN in the intimate, EVEN WHERE those old essentials (love, etc) are, where they took root /

it can be put this way: that it is not a question of loss or of a lack of love (of capability) but a deep and profound difference of the way this thing gets itself expressed, nowadays. Confronted by rot on all hands yet still active enough to want to go ahead—to undo that rot—those who are front dispose themselves toward the intimate just as aslant and acocked as they do toward all those other realities, external mostly, which are moving so curiously fast and treacherously before the nose that why? anywhere? let a twig break?

Love, as they have it, is as dead as peace, as war is. There is one requirement, only one requirement, anywhere (and what's so different about it, actually, from what the predecessors made so much of, with that word of theirs, that word amor plus how-they-figured-it-ought-to-behave)—the clue: open, stay OPEN, hear it, anything, really HEAR it. And you are IN.

You are all, all of you, so glib about what is human, so goddamn glib. Take a look. Just open your eyes, as he did, the Man who died:

1: the day of my interference is done
2: compulsion, no good; the recoil kills the advance
3: nothing is so marvellous as to be alone in the phenomenal world which is raging and yet apart

7

Washington to Brooklyn
28 October 1950 (postmark)

sat

frances: got thrown, by that last letter (stupid of me, just, that you thought i was shooting for you on "loneliness" "aloneness"—i couldn't see how i could disengage you (or myself) from such a notion

of course it is gun for gun, but not, frances, *at* you (as you yrself know, you *do* have yr shape, *are* yr shape) when we fire (when we fire gun to gun with anyone) it is not *at*, it is *from*   And *abt*, isn't it?

You are a big lady, and what you stand for (*where* you take yr stand—what you *are*) is of such moment to me (or what was the bizness all abt) that I must (in this sense only) (in the sense in which you took my Lawrence piece to be aimed *at* you) I must take you on (which means no more than that, we shape each other by the shapings of ourselves, no?)

> (Of course I understand, when you say, you cannot be alone anytime, anywhere. That's implied in any position of person & power (yrs, Christ's or DHL or my own effort)
>
> (And tho i take it you read DHL incorrectly—that is, that, he does not interpret the death of the Xfiction as necessary to the condition of the Man as he is in his story. On the contrary. But that you should see the Xfiction *yr* way—look I have absolute respect for that conceiving (that only by the death & xfictions, can you)

ONLY. No. I say no. I don't think. (And don't, please, get riled. For I know such a "No" is a big one, to you, for you. But remember: gun to gun, that's the trouble (for did you not say, how small you are o, how not human?) See, now, what I was working from—in that letter which emerged as the piece called THE ESCAPED COCK? I was just setting out a way I see it, against (& not at) (but, even more than against, *from* … a la. ta.

One grave shame. A Boston mag was borning. Was going to give 40 pages of first issue to none other—40, count em!—40. Verse, prose, & fragments (letters etc.) A fine idea. Solid. But, now, after much promising, and much, necessary, scrapping, looks as though the dope (the editor) will have to be socked / on nose—& with same sock, sure will go (will go gd ego) the 40 pages! (Fascinated me, a *Boston* mag: 1st since Emerson's Dial, i do believe!) Attrition, frances, attrition.[6]

Do write, when you can. And I'll (now that I've driven over that jam) make more of a letter to you. Do hope all is well (won't you please feel able to tell me, how things are going, work etc.?)

Love,

Charles

6 Olson was in the midst of a confrontation with Cid Corman over the direction of the planned *Origin* magazine.

8

Washington to Brooklyn
11 November 1950 (postmark 11 November 1950)

Saturday
Nov 11

frances—

sort of figure you will be looking for a letter from me monday

and do not want you to be disappointed

got dragged off on other business, today, when intended to answer you

will Monday say

hope all is well

love
Charles

9

Washington to Brooklyn
13 November 1950 (postmark 13 November 1950)

monday november 13 1950

frances: i do not think i shall say anything abt that last letter of yrs, unless you want me to. for it is a wholesale job, wasn't it, and i think you are too big a girl not to know what it was. (crazy thing: for you to abandon all yr own hard-won positions. And that i, (specifically I, not your other arrogation) fed off you, as you put it, well, what, frances motz, should, by yr own wisdom, be more wonderful? what?

Having done so (which means that you were such that it could be that beautiful) and having, admittedly, on one sector of the whole business not done well myself, I push silence at you, a nice silence, a good feeling. For you have made me proud.

One thing, tho: I happened to send off trinacria, a couple of days after yr letter came, to Germany, for translation & appearance there, under its new title, triskele. And it came in strong, as I was copying it, the question: who, who does frances think wrote that poem? who?

You see, girl, that you say you feel no longer in touch, that you raise yrself up and with such dogmatism, such doctrine of purity, expel me from that holyland of rimbaud, blake, & michel-ange-LO (lo! you!)—really, frances, isn't it, a wash-out, that you, who, by ishmael, sd, lo, olson …

what is it, frances?

do you think to pay me off, to punish me?

good lawd, girl, any man who's at his job (any of those men, i wld just hazard) has to do what he is, and does it, without such reference, does it, straight, between you and me, say, NOT soweiter (the fact is, if you want a literary allusion, what you sd only makes me very much of Alyosha Karamazov's persuasion, how he found (one seems to find) one takes one's human companions:

"won't let you climb
my apple tree, you can't slide
my cellar door")

That you should put it anyway—as who fails who, or whatever—frances: what was that word, Russian had no word, for (what words, such legislations)?

No, girl. I don't want to scold, back. Don't want to. Things are so much fatter, richer (you are) than you make yrself, when, as in that instance (o lady motz, take us up, in scale,—or, better, remind yrself, of yr *own* scale, of how life, it is, to be recognized

For no matter how you (understandably?) cry down, cry down, no matter how much this little body has given you such disappointment you say: look—the guy who wrote trinacria & ishmael is this guy. Now: you can't join the two facts, your way, that is, you can't say, how he did that and how he does this. He did one. He is disappointment or, he is still who. Look and see, dear one. And let me know.

Love,
Charles

10

Washington to Brooklyn
17 November 1950 (postmark 17 November 1950)

friday
nov 17
50

frances: Had the sweetest dream of you last night, in which so many of yr ways & gestures, shyness plus pride plus plunge re-enacted themselves—it was at some sort of resort, perhaps, and it was accidental we both came there separately, and I spotted the house you were in, and, as cautiously and shyly as you answered my (same) passing by (excitedly, both)—you raising yr arm hesitantly behind the curtains, I came in, to find a house-load of people, and, you, giving me the bizness, with a guy whose name was (Geoffrey) Mammon (the last, definitely!), I was all for walking straight through the door at the end of the passageway you two were going ahead of me down, I was so mad!

I'm sure that was a very stupid letter you had from me, this week. I'm sure it was.

It is so stupid, you and I, should, like this, be scratching. I deeply miss, the communication.

Seems so unimaginative, and fixed, that, such as you and me can't, go ahead. I buck you, no question, know that. And know I'm hard, as you sd, cold, frances (how was it you put it, set against you, was it, on and off?)

Don't want to labor it. Just, that, I feel most close to you, and like that, and wish, from that, we might go on.

Of course I don't know how to erase yr sense I was dishonest, by word & deed. Was. No argument. Allowed myself to be, overextended. And, my nature such, the moment, I do that, and come up against consequences thereof, am a nasty animal. (But don't, Frances, leave out of that account, that, it was, the over-extension, because, you are so close to me.)

Well, anyhow, here we are. And write, when you can, how you are,—hope, all is well, the job, Lucinda, yrself: HOW *are* you?

love,

Charles

11

Washington to Brooklyn
5 December 1950 (postmark 5 December 1950)

tuesday dec 5

frances:

curious that, when as i sd last letter, you are so very much as i imagine you shall never cease to be, to me, that, I do not write to you

it is a most strange time, any way

i think it is that, rather than anything else, that caused me to delay, answering, your suggestion, I join you, at Eliz.'s, tho, surely, I had to decide. so do not, please, frances, put any weight on it, particularly, that i do not think i will. for it is of no more import than, that, just now, i don't do anything, literally, anything

it is what i mean, by, how strange a time it is, how, strange (i sd to you, i had to fall back, but, i never guessed, i did not guess what, that meant)

nor is this cryptic. nor of import that i say no more. it is actually, a condition, a state nor is it unfruitful it is only that it is without issue, just now

and that i am bold, and let time go, and let this note be what it is to stand as a sign, would seem to me to be as well a sign of, how, i take it, you are so deeply a part of me, that you are, in my crazy self, all the full fact you ever were

which is why i can, so
exactly, send you

love,

Charles

12

Washington to New York[7]
11 December 1950 (postmark 11 December 1950)

mon dec 11

frances! why, capetown, that is "again"? or did i miss previous plan? tell me abt capetown, as of, you—as against rooshia, say, or, the States! (i mean, beside, what i can figure: any extras? say, like, oh, as you or i might go to iran for, altogether not contemporary or, future, reasons?)

this is a fast note, to catch the 5 o'c, to reach you tomorrow, to tell you, i am posting, registered, das buch,[8] from the p.o. (the problem, the p.o., for same)

and to tell you that, that things are reversed, as you say, doth not in the calyx-least, surprise this, citizen: good lord, lady, you & i know … And that the others, the fools, catch up? Well … But if you are glad, i am. And why shouldn't you be?

(As of here, at least, today, he is also, perkier)

((No particular good reason, either. Or is it that, all of us, crow, when, we have, the very little, overcome our incoherence? Even to a phrase? Or the world?))

Gay for you, girl, of joy,

Charles

7 This letter is addressed to Mrs. Frances Boldereff, A.S. BARNES, Publishers, 101 Fifth Avenue, New York 3, N.Y.

8 Olson returns Boldereff's "May 1936" notebook with his next letter.

13

Washington to Brooklyn
18 December 1950 (postmark 19 December 1950)

frances:

damndest thing, but, thursday, found out i could pick up 2 bills, from U.S.G., now, that, previously, was locked up (pension moneys), until age 65! So, tomorrow, shove off, bus, for mexico, and, hopefully, yucatan

(nor shld the bracket, any more than the
notebook, shld you, give it, any special
weight, frances: is event, in course, as,
for example, the, above, accident, say,
admitting, of course, the

will to get away from the worn-out frame, the U.S. (was it not, who sd, since 1928, the: L'univers concentrationnaire).

fact is, am very glad to get chance to (if moneys make it) to take that sun. don't figure it can last long, a month, maybe. Nor where. But will let you know

need it, no doubt

crazy difficult, to say, things like, hope all is well, you, and, the season (for you) Christ's, and lucinda, but do, frances, and please, take it, firm, from, this lad

love.

charles

12/18/50

Oh, yes, just in bad case,
let me enclose, registered
receipt, notebook.

Part Two

21 APRIL 1952–20 NOVEMBER 1952

Connie Olson was pregnant during the Yucatán months, and Kate Olson was born on 23 October 1951 after their return to Black Mountain College. New fatherhood absorbed Olson, but after six months of it he is looking out again, specifically to Brooklyn. In an unpublished letter to Connie (at Storrs), Olson said he never wanted to live with Boldereff, but he found it impossible to say finis to the affair. With this confession behind him, Olson turns immediately to the letter that begins this section (no. 14, 21 April 1952), which is a love letter composed entirely in objective correlatives. Boldereff replies (we have her letters again) with a feminine feint and questions of explication which soon bring him to an open declaration (no. 16, 17 May 1952).

The resurrection proceeds, and there is an actual visit to Brooklyn on the weekend of 28–29 June 1952, a "heady" occasion (no. 20, 3 July 1952). There may have been other visits, but it was the one in early October 1952 that proved a turning point (no. 25, 10 October 1952). Connie left Olson alone in their Washington house, where they had gone to spend the fall, on leave from Black Mountain. She took Kate with her to the college in a sort of trial separation. Strangely, this did not prompt Olson to rush into Boldereff's arms. Quite the contrary. While he pens a few short notes to Brooklyn (nos. 26, 27, 28, 30, 31), Olson is actually writing long letters to Connie, practically every hour of every day, thereby recording a formidable mid-life crisis, which ends only in his joining Connie and Kate at Black Mountain in December 1952. This life crisis shared with Connie undoubtedly explains the gap in letters between parts two and three.

RM

180 Clinton Street, Brooklyn, New York, contemporary photograph
courtesy Lucy Wilner

14

Washington to Brooklyn[1]
21 April 1952 (postmark)

Wash Monday

Frances:

It is your life I embrace and—what is so very beautiful—it is by your life that I feel embraced.

This, surely, is union.

It led on this way:

sex is the sun of the body. So, it is required of man and woman that we treat it as we would treat the sun, if we thought about it—that there would be no life in its absence.

Certainly something of this "logic" was what led peoples at some times to "worship" the sun, at least to remind themselves of the sun's potency, by acts of respect of it—that potency's effects upon them and upon their earth.

Equally certainly sexual energy is absolutely the measure of the amount of life in a human being, & is in the sky of him or her, however obscured, so long as he or she is alive (with this corollary, not now enough observed, that any number of people, and a surprising number, are not necessarily alive because they walk and talk)

So, to these clues:

(1) If the body is the earth—and other materials—on which sex shines, then the state of the body—the beauty of it—shall depend upon the potency of the source of its light and heat, however that source may shift north and south of equator; or go away on one side in order to shine twelve hours on another side (thus its apparent absences by its presence in another half); or by occlusions(?)—our equivalents of rain, cloud, volcanic dusts, coolings from winds, hazes from heat, etc.

1 Letter addressed to 180 Clinton Street, Brooklyn, New York.

(2) But the body calls for work on itself just as surely as the earth does, that it bear, even though it will, naturally. The real question—of human culture as the equivalent, as it properly is in each of us, of agriculture—is: what do you want your soil to bear, what crop. To the best of the farmers the question will be, what are the most useful crops, what are the ones will feed others and yet keep the soil fresh, make it even more productive?

(3) This work, then—this choice—is something in between the body as natural and the sun of itself, its natural sun. This is what is so very beautiful, that, though natural, what is produced—what a man or a woman, in the end, is—is the result of his or her own labor and his or her own care. This labor and this care require two things: the action of our selves (and, sometimes, a neighbor) and respect for our own element (this, ultimately, is a solitary act).

It, therefore, should surprise no one that the degree of the labor and the care is the measure of the degree of the crop, that is, given the earth and the sun to begin with, that is, given man and woman's respect for their own earth and its sun in a degree equal to that respect (or "worship", as above, which implies, surely, a sacredness to what is worshipped) for both the earth and the sun and certain winds, or whatever rains which those have who have obeyed the real reality that each of us implicitly is, and explicitly can be in touch with.

The embrace,

Charles

15

Brooklyn to Black Mountain[2]
4 May 1952 (postmark)

Charles—

The day your letter came I found in the library a poem of Rimbaud's the first—the "Credo in Unam" with a new title—the one he changed it to—

Le Soleil and Le Chair—"the sun and the flesh"

a perfect response to your letter—I saw the poem at noon—the letter at night—

I use so much energy during the day—I am no longer a letter writer—

the response between us is going to be slower—and be a matter of presences—I give terrific attention to my work—I told you it is like preparing for D-Day on a small scale—you cannot relax—I consider these few years as belonging to Lucinda—then I hope I will be free

So—I am slowly progressing with your poem—what comes to me is good—I do not understand the Old Man[3]—would you care to give me a hint—

Frances

2 This is the first surviving letter from Boldereff after the break.

3 Boldereff is referring to Olson's poem "To Gerhardt, There, Among Europe's Things of Which He Has Written Us in His 'Brief an Creeley und Olson'" published in *Origin* 4 (Winter 1951–52) and *Collected Poems*, pp. 212–22.

16

Black Mountain to Brooklyn
17 May 1952 (postmark 17 May 1952)

BMC May 17 52

Frances:

I have just this moment finished a sort of twin piece to what I sent you from Washington, but just because it is not so pure—does not have that simplicity I want (as I told you)—I shall not bother you with it, shall throw it into the folder in which such things which do not come off because I am not down to where a man has to be, go.[4]

You see, my lady, it is so tremendously beautiful that I do gauge—that I do have you (that you are that huge person that you are) that I have you to live with, that this (what you called the response between us) is of the order that those nights, meals, walks, hours proved again.

It stays so alive, all of what has gone between us. (It came out this way, instead of in another EPIGON:[5]

Woodward, Tarrytown, Woodward, Brooklyn.)

I find it very difficult to say this is not a poem as the other was!—though as of this "poem" (WTWB) I am sure that no one but you and I could recognize it, even as I am sure some will recognize EPIGON as the poem it is, one day ((just so you may know how I love you, I wish to say I have never for an instance lost the delicacy of how you put it, that EPIGON might not see the light of print, it was so intimate; it will, whenever.))

I am no longer a letter writer, either. (Two days ago it was a 16 hour day, and only four it of my only proper own.) But that is not the essential reason: it is also for me too as you put it there, a matter of presences.

4 Presumably "He in the dark stall" dated 17 May 1952, in *Collected Poems*, pp. 265–68.

5 "Epigon" is the poem Olson wrote after their first meeting in November 1949.

And I, for my part, will come to you just as soon, and as often, as I can make it possible.

Permit me to add this: that your "presence," in the other sense, in me, is a living delight—& beauty (no matter how much that is not the equal of what WTWB is, was—and life bless us—may be).

Charles

About Old man: it is an archaism, in the deepest & widest image sense, and though I know what it is in one way, I feel so strongly that the poem is what it is because that thing is buried in it—is the source of the life of it—then do, my darling, let it stay no more named & disclosed than it is, there

as you know we have to, the thing, when we have it in our hand

17

Woodward to Black Mountain
1 June 1952 (postmark 2 June 1952)

[letterhead: Woodward Inn]

Sunday morning

Charles dear—

We had a family reunion at mother's over Memorial Day and I have brought Lucinda here for the summer—

This morning I was reading Shakespeare *Henry the VIII* in bed and the resemblance of *Moby Dick* struck me so forcibly (in the rhythms and feel of the language) that I wondered no one until you had come upon it.

I picked up just before I left New York and had time only to smell, a new book on Melville my guess is you and I will both approve—*Spirit from the Dust* by Ronald Mason an Englishman—done in a big spirit and from what I can see at a quick glance has never heard of Olson. I think your publishers have hunted in the wrong market and my guess is if you were to send Mason one, he would eat your book with delight—since he seems at great pains to want to prove the *size* of the man—if you want to borrow my copy after I have read it—let me know. I am working like a demon—at Doubleday—takes me several days in the country to relax enough to notice how tired I am!—will travel all night and go straight to work tomorrow morning.

How long will you be in Black Mountain?

Frances

18

Black Mountain to Brooklyn
17 June 1952 (postmark 19 June 1952)

June 17

Frances:

This has come to my hand ahead of its first publication (apparently found among mss.)[6] and as it absolutely belongs to you I send it on, without waiting on myself. (Last winter I took on the job of chairing the committee for the summer session here, and though I shall not work the first four weeks of it, I have had, somewhat, to see it through its opening, next Wednesday, the 25th. After that, I shall be free. So if you want to get any word to me after receiving this, write to me Washington—in case I can get away earlier, and am in transit.)

It was, you will know, something to have a letter from you from Woodward!

It is called RESURRECTION OF THE FLESH.

Oh then be nameless and be never seen!
And speak no syllable, and never be
Even thought of!—but between
Your nothing and my nothingness, touch me!

They should never have given you names, and never, never
Have lent you voice, nor spoken of the face
That shone and darkened. They were all too clever.
Now let it all be finished! leave no trace!

Reveal us nothing! roll the scripts away!
Destroy at last the heavy books of stone!
Kill off the Word, that's had so much to say!
And show us nothing! leave us quite alone!

6 Presumably Olson acquired this D.H. Lawrence poem through Monroe Engel of Viking Press, publishers of Lawrence's *Collected Poems*.

Go, go away, and leave us not a trace
Of any Godhead, leave us in the dark!
And let the dark be soundless, without face
Or voice or any single spark

Of what was God! Be gone, be utterly gone!
Relieve us now of all remembrance even
Of what was godly! Leave us quite alone
Within the silence, void of echoes even.

Oh, it is finished! I would like to take
My garments off, but all, even memory,
And what I've understood, and the utter ache
Of everything I've known, even dreamily.

To take it off, this clothing of a man,
This content of my consciousness, this very me
Which I am still and have been all I can
And am and was, shed it all thoroughly.

To come at last to nothingness, and know
Nothing and nothing any more, and so
Not even dream, not even pass away
Nor cease to be: dark on the darkness stay.

And then within the night where nothing is,
And I am only next to nothingness,
Touch me, oh touch me, give me destinies
By touch, and a new nakedness.

I want to know no more. I want to see
Not anything, nor ever again ask: "Why?"
I let the whole thing go! Still there is me!
Touch me then, touch me, I did not die!

Upon the wincingness of next to nothingness
That I am now, Ah, lay one little touch
To start my heart afresh! Give me the soft, small stress
Of just one touch! Even so, do I ask too much?

He must have done this about the time of THE ESCAPED COCK, don't you think? And though I miss those sorts of things in this, yet there are beautiful things here, are there not? I shall be eager to hear you on it. It is a beautiful thing

Frances,

Charles

19

Washington to Brooklyn
26 June 1952 (postmark)

thursday

frances:

figure me for 6:00 Saturday[7]

(that wld be by

express bus.

but allow me this spread—of

the Congressional, arriving 7:30, in case

THIS VERY WICKED HEAT is still pouring itself down (it is reported to be easing Friday

never in my life did i feel anything like this heat—incredible: makes me feel that if it goes up one more notch we are all fried bugs on this plate of an earth beat on by a sun going amok. Crazy sense, that, between ice and fire …

to tell you,

love,

c

7 Olson was in Brooklyn for the weekend of 28–29 June 1952.

20

Washington to Brooklyn
3 July 1952 (postmark 4 July 1952)

Wash July 3

Frances:

Tuesday & Wednesday I went to *every* bookstore in this spread out small town—and no luck in the hand. But the bookstore I felt sure would have the Rimbaud could order it (they claimed). And so I have. They say ten days.

Am anxious to see my daughter and Con.[8] So will make a run down there tomorrow. Will let you hear from me as soon as I am back here. (It probably means I will miss meeting Helen.)

It has not been good here: Black Mt business was back on my doorstep Wednesday morning. And Moore[9] is unbearable—so raw (skinless from some assumptions of his dramas as more important than dirt & smells) that I find myself looking away, as one does from what hurts one's eyes, as one does from vulgarities and stupidities. So I have arranged that he be gone before I come back. (And whether I shall buy is very much on my mind.)

I think you know from my face how heady it was, there, with you, no?

Love,
Charles

8 Connie was now the registrar of Black Mountain College and resident there. Olson was using the Washington house during his semester off.

9 Composer Frank Moore was subletting the Washington house and remained there until September 1952.

21

Black Mountain to Brooklyn (special delivery)
5 July 1952 (postmark 5 July 1952)

July 5

Just a note, Frances, to tell you this:

> riding the bus hard, it dawned on me that to give *is* the whole damned thing, that it does mean all you've got, and that it is the way one asks nothing of anyone except such a like act of self, that this *is* the way the ego withers

Which will be no news about life to you, but it comes at me as an illumination only comparable to that sun go, April[10]

And I wanted you to have it. (The moment it broke over me I heard yr phrase truly for the 1st time—"for free"

You do give,

love

C

10 Olson is referring to his letter of 21 April 1952 (no. 14).

22

Black Mountain to Brooklyn
16 July 1952 (postmark 17 July 1952)

Wed July 16

Frances:

To keep you on—I am working, and so, stay put. In fact, I am trying to see if I can sell the rest of them the idea of my getting myself a substitute for the promised second four weeks.

No word yet that your Rimbaud has been received. But the moment I hear, if I am not back in Wash., I'll have them send it direct to you, just because you are on. (The others I renewed to July 28)

I have the deepest feeling of enrichment by you.

Charles

23

Black Mountain to Brooklyn (telegram)
25 July 1952

FRANCES BOLDEREFF
180 CLINTON ST

JUST REALIZED RIMBAUDS DUE WASHINGTON MONDAY.
PLEASE WIRE RANDOLPH PLACE CARE FRANK MOORE.
LOVE CHARLES

24

New York to Washington
26 September 1952

[letterhead: Doubleday & Co.]

Friday 26th

Charles—

I had a brief but highly satisfactory meeting with Arabella Porter on Wednesday—she said the head editor was in England—would be back on the fourth of October—she could not give me a definite answer until he comes—I suggested a separate volume on the dance—different from their book on *Ballet*—something including what you might call a philosophic approach to dance in relation to life—

The young people here are literally mad for Apollonius[11]—several would like to buy, if you have any copies for sale—and our reader has suggested another advance guard publisher if Signet or Mentor do not use it.

Please drop me a note as to where you want Miss Porter to contact you if the thing goes through.

Frances

11 Olson's dance-play *Apollonius of Tyana* had been published at Black Mountain College in September 1951.

25

Washington to Brooklyn[12]
[c. 10 October 1952]

Regret so no answer your phone tonight. First to ask your pardon astonishing silence wonderful business Apollonius. Fact is, I wanted long battle of Black Mountain over and to be in live touch with you again. May I see you tomorrow. Will phone ahead.

Love

12 This note, handwritten on the back of Boldereff's letter, is the draft of a telegram presumably sent, paving the way for a visit. This is likely the visit that precipitated Connie's leaving Washington for Black Mountain in a trial separation on 17 October 1952.

26

Washington to Brooklyn (postcard)
23 October 1952 (postmark)

Thurs.

Frances:

Big news (in mails today) is: I have the Pleiade Rimbaud for you! (Crazy. Went to Whyte's yestiddy, & got same blankness. But apparently, after I left, they found they had filled my order on Sept. 10! And so informed me by mail today.

I shall pick it up shortly—& bring it with me when I come.

Shortly O

Charles

Love to L—
fr the Russian General, Pants

No word yet from Riboud

27

Washington to Brooklyn
6 November 1952 (postmark)

Thurs

Frances—

It doesn't look good for this weekend at the moment. King went too early for me—& as I am going like a house a fire, it is not at all wise to stop, even for (what I woke up Monday with my mouth, & me, full of

"the lineaments of"

Just to give you a present report. And to give you my word

Charles

I shall phone you, or something
—or just arrive, & take
my chances, if the drive
stops (if the other drive …

28

Washington to Brooklyn (postcard)
13 November 1952 (postmark)

Thurs

All things fine. But this run is such a salmon—so thick of fish—I continue to let it come.

Just so you know.

C

29

New York to Washington
17 November 1952 (postmark)

[letterhead: Doubleday & Co.]

Charles dear—

I wonder if you would be kind enough to send back the Mason *Spirit from the Dust*. I can sell it to Barnes & Noble.

Am delighted the catch is so good!

Lucinda baptized yesterday—read her own responses with most beautiful gravity—everyone charmed—

Frances

Where is *Origin* (VI)?

30

Washington to Brooklyn
19 November 1952 (postmark 19 November 1952)

Wed Nov 19 52

Frances—

If I'd known you'd sell! Please let enclosed be what Barnes & Noble ... I am so happy to have it for my own collection[13]

And *such* greetings to you who ...

Ought to be *out* soon.

The man who was, plus
whoever he is

O

& tell Lucinda
I shall get her a
whole *box* of Turkish delight,
for her confirmation

13 The copy of Ronald Mason's *The Spirit Above the Dust: A Study of Herman Melville* (London: John Lehmann, 1951) remained in Olson's library. He initiated an extensive correspondence with Mason, beginning in April 1953.

31

Washington to Brooklyn
20 November 1952 (postmark 20 November 1952)

Thurs.

FM:

a new one (written to you, another "translation":

FROM THE INCA[14]

The mighty man, and the mother-egg,
leg over leg over leg

Charles

14 "From the Inca" remained unpublished until *Collected Poems*, p. 275.

Part Three

14 MAY 1953–11 AUGUST 1954

In March 1953 Olson was tremendously engaged with a three-week seminar he had organized at Black Mountain College, the Institute of the New Sciences of Man. He might have been freer to respond to Boldereff's cry of despair in the first letter of this section had he not taken up with Betty Kaiser, a music student at the college. The compartmentalizing of Olson's life in this period is demonstrated by his growing connectedness to Boldereff and his persistence in these letters, no matter what else is going on in his life. Arthur Rimbaud is the figure who connects them here. Boldereff's disquisitions on "Credo in Unam" and Olson's reverence constitute a high point in these later letters.

RM

32

Brooklyn to Black Mountain
14 May 1953 (postmark)

180 Clinton Street
Brooklyn 1, New York

Charles—

At this moment I open by chance the letter with the poem *Resurrection of the Flesh* and it seems absolutely perfect—says everything that Spengler et al could say—

I am in a desperate situation—have been ruthlessly fired—absolutely no money—

But more than that, desperate to see a sane human being who has a soul and understands something.

If you possibly can, come as soon as you can—I have been waiting for you for a long time—(I mention that today in my possession I have literally 25c which Lucinda earned and gave me—and one week's salary in bank which is my total capital—my debts mountainous!)

Will say I did not write because every week I thought next week

1. You would come

2. I would have news that Doubleday had taken your book.[1] The editor was crazy about it and his reader was crazy about it—said it was a "must"—do not know if the delay is caused by the fact of having 12 titles out (in works before yours got to him) and they may want to see how the series goes before spending any more money. There are 12 titles now out. He has not yet returned the book to me—I am on very good terms with him—so if anything breaks he will surely let me know. (The idea has occurred to me that the economics in it may be anti-Doubleday!)

Frances

1 Boldereff has proposed a reprint of *Call Me Ishmael* for the new Anchor paperback series.

33

Black Mountain to Brooklyn
16 May 1953 (postmark 16 May 1953)

Sat May 16

Frances:

Yr very bad news in—and please don't take it as anything that I don't immediately come, or put my quarter in as Lucinda has. Just keep keeping me on, to how it goes. And let me figure.

This is merely to console you, & to urge you not to panic over the money question. Or to grind over the firing. For you know those birds, that they do it every time, & just such clean work as you do can only be left alone in an *independent* situation.

(All the rest—my silence, absence, stiffness etc.—is merely more of same. And need not trouble you.

((The thing is, it is enough, that it troubles me! The plain "hurts" of it make me so sick I wrote you a letter two & a half months ago. Which I destroyed. Simply that ... christ!

Charles

34

Black Mountain to Brooklyn
25 May 1953

wed may 25

frances:

i have the enclosed,[2] anyway, to send you—and i pray it may find a welcome with you (as obviously my last letter didn't). It will have failings, too (as the letter obviously did); but I want it to give you pleasures, in spite of all the hurts I seem to be as expert in as the enemy. (It's crazy, how any book of mine can never be as *Ishmael* was, simply, that we have known each other: it's as crazy as, for the same reason, I cannot be a friend, in that easy sense, just because you mean to me what you do.)

(because i didn't come, and didn't have damned cent to send you, i didn't thank you for giving *Ish* the ride you have given it with those Anchor people

but you will guess i do (even if the book is, as any old book, over the dam; and even if i hardly expect to be allowed in, to such publication—DHL is as far as they are likely to go (tho the sales on the "Studies" shall surprise them, I bet
(but by now it shld be called, not "Studies," but "Sex & Allegory in Classical Am Literature":

only his Whitman, stands up

what i think you will be pleased to know, is, that two other books are just abt ready to go to press. And I'll have for you in three to four months. A prose letters (MAYAN LETTERS, fr the same printers as the enclosed). And more poems (1–10 of THE MAXIMUS POEMS) fr Stuttgart!

2 *In Cold Hell, In Thicket*, published as *Origin* 8 in April 1953. The magazine is inscribed "for frances with love charles" (Frances Boldereff Papers, Archives and Special Collections, University of Connecticut, Storrs).

(The place of the latter publication pleases me no end, just that, Germany, was where the biz (so far as Western Europe & us goes) did kick off, wasn't it?

And what you taught me (by yr Penn State catalogue) I was just ten minutes ago drawing on, to lecture this Stuttgart publisher & designer abt space—and abt quietness, & intensity:

he shows all the wolf-wolf of modern art presses; and I'm frightened he'll make a howl of the maximus things. And it's rough, when you are, as a writer, so loud as I am, not to have modest clothes to wear!
It was a nice feeling to lecture him according to the practice of, yrself!

Charles

35

Brooklyn to Black Mountain
1 June 1953 (postmark)

Charles—

I am very excited at the new volume—it happens that this very morning I am reading a very exciting "Communications No. 12" from The Oriental Institute of University of Chicago

"The Alphabet—Its Rise and Development from the Sinai Inscriptions" by Martin Sprengling[3]

this is so marvelous—the bird caught at last—the actual first alphabet—caught—the booklet written by an American with humor, earnestness, intellect—*first rate stuff* get and read.

My mind is flowing so fast these days I am ready to begin my own book—but will probably have to delay for another three years or so—

"La Chute" belovéd by me—fits in perfectly with readings about the people who invented the alphabet who called themselves "belovéd of Balat"—a goddess—I think the moment is gathering where the heaviness of 3000 years of Hebrew and Catholic tradition which have weighed us down, is breaking up—where man will steadfastly gain belief in joy—as portrayed among other places by John—whose Fourth Gospel I am now studying about in a very scholarly book—and so many, many ancient prejudices falling off one by one—for instance under the most careful modern scholarship. The woman taken in adultery was originally the woman of many sins—quite possibly not adultery at all—and the point of the story seems to be—no *man* can judge—only God is permitted to judge *anyone*.

I will examine the book in minute detail—am very pleased about the two others—I have as yet no knowledge about a job—so keep in close

3 University of Chicago Press, 1931. Olson later invited Sprengling to Black Mountain College.

touch as I am leaving here the end of the month—no money—and have no idea between N.J., Pa., N.Y. where I will be—

I did not answer your letter because to a person in my desperate situation it said one simple word "No."—I did not do anything about it inside at all—when you are looking for bread—and a door is closed—you search for another one—in this case my sister—who has lent me $450.00 and even that does not cover my need—I am thinking of taking a job as a housekeeper—

Frances

As I glance through it looks very fine—

"Knowing all ways"

"For Sappho, Back" (absolute beauty)

Have not seen the others—pages not cut—

Hope you have not changed "At Yorktown" which I loved the way it was.

36

Brooklyn to Black Mountain
2 June 1953 (postmark)

Charles—

I write you on this paper[4] which is deeply mine because the flower I found in a lonely brook in Woodward—in dazzling, lonely, morning light, wading, holding up my skirts—and was awestruck—its brilliance, alone there—

I write to tell you a book does come to me as once before—*is* perhaps the very visit I needed—

I write to tell you you have written three poems—

In Cold Hell, In Thicket is the greatest statement in our times of our world in any form—

For Sappho, Back is absolute and will long endure

La Torre is also perfect and completes *In Cold Hell*

All the new ones are manly—real men's poetry

A Round
&
A Canon   is perfect too

I sit in my soul too thrilled to move a finger or to speak—I walk over crackling leaves without a sound—I await as I have awaited (thought it would take you at least 10 years) and can see that the flow—backwards forwards—of the pain of these years—in and out—has wrought you—who have still acres of miles to cover but you will one day come to my "Hallelujah!" with Dostoyevsky et notres frères.

Rimbaud and I salute you
Saluté di cuore
Frances

4 Boldereff is using a card picturing a cardinal flower.

(There are a few words (I do not say where) that are as beautiful as any words since God permitted Word to man and you are greeted by all my family who at this moment, smile. S.B., J, R, M, V.)[5]

May I say that the last line of 2 in *La Torre* is not necessary—does not at all sound like you and should just be omitted—

If you feel there must be a line make it an Olson line and put it as 3.

5 These initials likely refer to Sergei Boldereff, Joyce, Rimbaud, Michelangelo, and Villon.

37

Black Mountain to Brooklyn
17 June 1953 (postmark)

You mustn't ever mind my silences, Frances. For you are *never* out of my mind.

I work peculiarly—and am forever struggling with achieving the edge each day requires: to teeter, where rhythm is.

So if I let time go by, please think of it as used. And also know I hear everything you say to me—indeed, wish the verse (and me) was as much as your *magnanimity* to same.

(And that I am scared of words to you—
that they be forever leaning over backwards, and do you no wrong.)

That you have found Sprengling (whose work has sent me, for two years), that you are into Herculaneum and Pompeii (where I haven't yet got), and that you have the Eisenstein for me: all this, of course, is as it has to be. This is the other place where we touch.

And you will know that the most astonishing thing you have said to me in these letters is, ten years! My god! You (literally) give me too much. I am not allowed that time.

And you will guess that the biggest damn thing of all, was that you did tell me Helen, was there for you, when you needed it.

And be sure, I have no comfort, in how I am.

I do pray all is not the worst. And please—keep me on.

Yrs,
Charles

38

Black Mountain to Brooklyn
1 July 1953 (postmark 1 July 1953)

July 1

Frances!

It just dawned on me (yesterday) that it was already the end of the month: please let me know if this does reach you / how you are / and where

The book came,[6] and though I haven't read it, the great thing is to have it so that, when, suddenly, he does return to my mind, I have it, to go to.

ICH is beginning to get attacks—& it is fortunate I have MAX as a buffer between.

Charles

On ISH, a thought struck me, the other day: if *Anchor* only had one objection (that it was too small) the thing could be made a "Studies in M," by addition of the NR two pieces, the WR thing on David Young, David Old; maybe the "Letter," with Mrs EMM taken out; plus a long recent poem called "The Collected Poems of" (written originally for an Eng. ed. of HM's verse, not now to be published). Think of it, anyway—if anything more comes of the Anchor idea.[7]

6 Marie Seton, *Sergei M. Eisenstein: A Biography* (New York: A.A. Wyn, n.d.). Olson's copy was inscribed by Boldereff and dated "Summer 1953."

7 Olson is proposing a *Studies in Melville* comprising *Call Me Ishmael* and later writings: "Materials and Weights of Herman Melville" in *New Republic* for 8 and 15 September 1952; "David Young, David Old" *Western Review* (Fall 1949); *Letter for Melville 1951* (Black Mountain College, 1951) with the addressee's name, Eleanor Melville Metcalf, deleted from the poem; and "The Collected Poems of," a poem unpublished until *Collected Poems*, pp. 278–82.

39

Brooklyn to Black Mountain
[4 July 1953]

Charles dear—

I have made a decision you will approve—I have hired myself out as a secretary to a very smart man—I receive $55 a week, which is nothing but it pays my rent and I am not trying to do anything now but keep the boat afloat. Business is practically non existent in the publishing world. My guess is that Anchor will not do *any* new titles until they see how the first twelve (chosen before I gave him *Ishmael*) will do—they have poured a lot of money into them and from what I hear around at booksellers and stuff, they are not very welcome—no one sees the idea—it has been tried by many different houses and America simply will not buy good books.

I thought you would have joy in the full, documented look of the Eisenstein book, with all those photos and his beautiful signature across the front cover—I knew it would be a long time before you would read it, but the book gives off a kind of joy—through the size of the man inside it.

I have been reading Rimbaud so closely, am so close to him it seems very hard for me to think he doesn't know me—Fowlie has put out a new book,[8] which is very wrong in certain ways—but which is very right in the total valuation and some of Fowlie's translations are superb—some are impossible. Nevertheless I learned that he was tall for sure—I found an anecdote from his youth and I have learned so many tiny, revealing things that it is as though I am literally Rimbaud in female form—the identity of our natures in all its bad as well as good points is so close.

I feel literally colossus—since I am lying low and *staying where I want to* and in defeating their whole destructive, hateful program of death-dealing to a person who is alive I feel that I have accomplished a real blow

8 Wallace Fowlie, *Rimbaud* (New York: New Directions, 1946), which Olson had previously used (*AMC*, no. 177, p. 276).

at their innards. How absolutely evil the whole imitative dead pattern of American business is only Rimbaud can say—

I have growled out to myself with deep satisfaction over and over again your phrase "refrigerator-ripened fruit" that whole essay is *good.*[9]

Frances

9 Boldereff is referring to the "Human Universe" essay in *Origin* 4 (Winter 1951–52): pp. 217–28.

40

Black Mountain to Brooklyn (postcard)
21 July 1953 (postmark 21 July 1953)

Jl 21

Frances:

Got caught in an argument on jazz and verse, and didn't get the intended letter written to you today. But this is to get some word to you, to tell you how good it is to have your letters, & to ask for more. I've been off the verse kick, but it doesn't matter, as it is inconstant, as Shelley knew!

Charles

41

Brooklyn to Black Mountain
[c. 27 August 1953]

180 Clinton Street
Brooklyn One, N.Y.

Charles,

I am now in the exact mood in which Melville draped his room in black and decided not to attempt communication, on account. It is unbelievable that the number of human beings who have any animation, any enthusiasm, any attempt to make a spiritual stab is so small that you simply can not find even one to talk to.

As usual, I end up in the library.

Anyway, I am again in a great flux as pertains to my plans. I have now forged a pretty tight picture as to what I want a year from now—the whole thing turns in my mind as to how to achieve what I want without murdering myself in the meantime.

I have noted two beautiful things recently, which indicate very much to me. In the magazine of I believe the New York Times was a story on returning G.I.'s from Korea, as to how they act. Their politeness, their absolute indifference, their eerie air of not hearing and not caring what it is you are saying to them, *although* they did a terrific job of fighting, flying, etc. I know this also as a personal thing in the case of my nephew. They just stare out the window and do not seem to be in the room where they are sitting.

This, plus the beautiful story in American Weekly about Ted Williams, who so obviously thinks and feels his fellowship with the men who were over there, and has his ideas about the whole thing we have here.

I feel sure that something very important is happening. That what you might call the sales angle of the modern world is losing ground, that those kids are still completely inarticulate as to what it is they want, but obviously, they know they have brothers and they know our setup is that you can't act that way. It is probably the most beautiful form of warfare that has yet happened—that eery quality of a man who has strung up a terrific record of flying and still is not a man killing himself to get back home and buy a deep freeze.

Frances

42

Black Mountain to Brooklyn
29 August 1953 (postmark 29 August 1953)

August 29th

Frances:

Thought to have had the new book of verse (Maximus, 1–10) to you by now. But the printer (Stuttgart, a Dr Cantz) was slow. It is now due, they say, middle of September (with announcement in it, as a flyer, of subscriptions wanted for Max #II: to be made up of Maximus Poems 11–22). 33 are now done. But until more are I shall not be sure 23 on, are set.

The whole thing is, I take it, another sort of verse. And I'm not at all sure you'll like it—more that sort of prosiness of the Melville Letter, say. But I am very damned anxious to have your word (even if it is as hidden as what you wouldn't tell me about *In Cold Hell!*)

One thing, though: I guess these Maximus "letters"—this poem—is the attempt to come to grips with this country which plagues us all, to try to run it down. And to get in just such elements of despair, & such men, as you voice in your letter to me last week (as well as you cried out to me that question, from Woodward, what, Olson, do you see in these States to excuse them, tell me)

Not that I can—decidedly. But I can say what I am stuck with. And surely, it isn't hope, anyway, that is an issue. It's the power of form, which is life. (That sentence suddenly writes itself spang into the midst of our old "argument," isn't it?!! (I still keep as a quote—& look at it, look at it—your magnificent cry (in letter abt Rimbaud / & sd Russkis) "a capacity for extremes and for taking for granted that living a thing is beyond measure more important and deeper than any other gesture of any kind"

Anyway, let me always say this: that your life is the proof. And whatever you meant (in yr last letter) about the year ahead—how to achieve it without hurting yourself in the meantime ... o, anyone of our isolations (those boys you speak of, or The Magnificent Splinter, as Williams is known in Boston)[10] is part, too, of the question.

Frances, Frances

Charles

10 Baseball player Ted Williams.

43

Black Mountain to Brooklyn
27 October 1953 (postmark 29 October 1953)

October 27

Frances:

A very damned bad time, and thus my stiffness, of no word to you (actually, yr own economics lays on me as, just now, the unbelievable hung state of this place (such debts, & only fifteen students, and have to sell land, to continue, or, dissolve), plus notice to vacate the Washington place for unpaid rent, the news that Ishmael went out of print a year ago—imagine those bastards not letting me know that that had happened—and that when suddenly Creeley's press—the Divers Press—is catching on with Marlboro books, Brentano's, and possibly even Doubleday, and he wants to up the edition of my MAYAN LETTERS from 400 to 750 to meet this new possibility of outlets, he don't have a cent more to put in

—and all this with a man living under me, exactly under me, who is worth untold millions![11]

it's wild, it's crazy, it's

life *on* a mountain, as well as under, at the damned moment of, these last five, months!

Look: i am in such bad state, that, just let me be wild, in this letter, that, I need to, not writing to you piling me up so (i don't write, simply, that, to see you makes the only sense), that, like today, when i must, or bust, i am not quite sane, you know

damned ground down, from, the past four years, say (a fine letter, i say, as of, date, Year IV, yes?

11 Paul Williams, student and patron, Black Mountain College.

and i wanting, planning, to have you MAX, as of, sd date. But those damned German printers have played light with Williams, the publisher; and the book (even my own first copy air mail) is not yet here—months late; and the news is that it will be late November before books arrive.

(I even didn't send you the most handsome announcement Williams made of it, that, i was expecting, daily, the damned thing itself

Plus (as of above distracted state, that, since June, the further "letters" of the Maximus Letters, have had me involved in one of the most difficult compositional times ever—done thru 22, solid, and mss ready since August, but, just at poem 23, even tho another fifteen at least done, I have stayed unsatisfied that the movement of the poem from that point is right

And it is "history" (and of my own front yard, Gloucester) which has had me engaged blindly stupidly

—yet know, have known, that, just here, 23, is the hump, of the book, however long, it may turn out to be (very exciting, actually, the whole force of, to do, a thing of, its problems

So write me, more often than you do, not letting my silences be a thing other than, as i tell you, it is, that, they are not the equal of:

and, that if you tell me i am a dwarf,[12] then, I am—appearances, notwithstanding

—as, say, another was, a
skylark?

For i believe you know, as you know—and, as i don't feel a salmon, then …

(but, if I appear to play, i don't, goddamn it—or at least am a nub enuf to refuse to

Miss *all* news. Please give it to me.

(Except for the Max's, only poem of any worth done is one called PROENSA,[13] which you shall see—

a break-through, as song, and on love, that, with another series of translations from the Provencal, I finally up and slammed that drag-arsing, that, those singers, then, were our superiors

that damned imposition of Pound's and others, of melopoeia

12 This comment is from a missing letter.

13 *Collected Poems*, pp. 291–93.

bah:

the thing to you, of eyes, and a salmon, say:
goddamn the notion that, us, can't sing of, and of wars, and: the state of the State

my job

(it is so stupid, for, Villon: who, like him, amongst, those rural celebrators?

cities, songs (rain-

bow, over

the span (the

present:

sang

i make
music

(and, Frances, you can imagine the joy of, to make words, sing, that song is in them as, we, speak 'em

(at which point you are the
dilemma, your claim of "life" versus

as, in my poem, it got to be
history versus—

as it damn well is

—art

(that what i know
between my thumb's pad, and my index finger's side, as of cod, is a discrepancy no history
of same can
equal

(the manner of above jagged placement of letter reminds me that the "Morning News" (if you remember?) is just out, in print,[14] and (by god)

still delighteth

me (will send you a copy as soon as i get 'em

14 The poem "Morning News" appeared in *Origin* 10 (Summer 1953).

(a sign, perhaps,
of what slowness—well, not to get into that, but, 10 years???????

("You say the damndest
things," he sd, walking, through the, house

And don't mind these commas: every
so often—and it is significant, a sort of stuttering!—i go into these
obstructings of, the flow of, sin-

tax

(and puns accompany same, as,

you will have,

noticed!

(where song—where does it—

lie? where? how does the fish

gleam?

(they lay along the beach,
gasping. And Boone and I, like
crazy, got gunny-sacks, and,
dragging them home in what is the only time of triumph except one other
time when
the leaves were as many
and yet i was as full of blood as this sack was of
hake, we cried, thinking
our parents
would be so very pleased

—and they tried to give them away, nobody
could use 'em

It's
any one of us who
matters

(and that is not easy,
when modernity
was what raised us

and vulgarity

14 May 1953–11 August 1954

was her children,

when all the world

went for it (Lady

Wishfort was,

as compared to,

these, a

goddess!

the loss of

the straightest (i know two

who are—and he,

by grace of,

the head of,

the tide

two,

out of,

all!

It does one

good

to hear from you. Yes. And maybe (now that my
distress is almost complete) i shall lose my
tongue, he sd, meaning
loose (what
he has
neglected

and if i speak in riddles,
it is because, today, i make
commas!

love, he sd: O!

Charles

44

Brooklyn to Black Mountain
28 October 1953

October 28, 1953

Charles dear—

I have now in front of me your "Human Universe" which I reread a few nights ago. I was deeply impressed. My mind, enlarged by a close study of Arthur Evans' *Palace of Minos at Knossos*, read this essay in its entirety or let us say—took in these words, for the first time.

I do not believe I told about my trip to Lewistown, where I rode with the Lithuanian seaman—and he said, in the definitely most different conversation I have ever had in my life, "I don't want another man's inspiration—no matter how wonderful it is"—referring to his refusal to read Melville or anyone else—he apparently only wants to study facts and to draw all his own conclusions. I wish I could convey the air he had about him of being absolutely alone—and one could see him day after day, thinking, somewhere aboard a vessel. He said fiercely, "I am a seaman because I like the sea" and he has "buddies." I was very pleased with him—he kept his male cool thing so separate and yet was so hot to get to a truth. I felt he worshipped Melville in a truer sense than any man I had ever met—at parting—he hesitated—told me his name—did not ask for mine and looking very into—said "Perhaps we shall meet again" and walked out so desperately separate and bound to it like a wife.

As I read Evans, who is so beautiful I am someday going to fork over the $150—to buy 5 volumes—I am conscious of where and how we moved off and I am certain as the stars, Charles—that we are coming back on—this is perhaps the single most exciting title, because Evans is such a scholar—and at the same time moved in a way he lets show once in a volume in one adjective—and the stuff, at one site, goes back layer after layer to Neolithic—and touches on all the provinces the archaeologists are investigating. The plates send me into ecstasy and I feel sure no more gorgeous people has ever lived. How we got shoved out of this cradle into the Semitic cradle I am here to say I don't know but am sure complaining about.

Apropos your essay—it satisfies me in its best sentence—I am pleased with "There must be a way which bears *in*." This is what I believe Bergson's whole message was and the reason I keep saying over and over that the Sappho poem is so absolute is because it does just that—it does not describe it is itself a tiny stretch of reality—a living event each time one encounters it that is never in any sense repeated. It is always a new living movement that encounters one with depths and unknowns, precisely as a human personality does. If anyone has done it before—I would name only Rimbaud.

I find the essay very good.

Frances

45

Brooklyn to Black Mountain
1 November 1953

Sunday–November 1–1953

Charles dear—

In a few days my sister's birthday and the anniversary of the day I got my job at Jersey City Print—and thus the beginning …

I was in bed when I wrote you Wednesday—very ill—all week—and Charles, this last month I have thought the boys had finally got me—I just felt sure I couldn't make it to year's end—but some electric transfer out of Minos took place and now I *know* that my long crucifixion is almost over—I know I shall be taken down from the cross and even petted and pampered—as yet, I have no hint as to details—but I thought I should pass the good word on to you.

I have also a hint that perhaps your long night of waiting is over—that the new Motz is ready again to give scrupulous attention to Olson and that in other ways you too will be rewarded for your long night of waiting. Again I have no hints as to details.

I have been reading each word with care of "The Gate and the Center"[15]—I now want to discuss in detail with you a few points of dating (after my long study of this Minoan stuff) but in general want to say that only on Friday I read with intense excitement *proof* in Evans of the exact statement you make "And I venture to say that their enlarged dimensions are no where as discrepant from them as we … would surmise"—Only two days ago I was screaming to Lucinda across the dinner table—it is all *true!* Theseus slew the Minotaur—the hero dove for and brought back the

15 Boldereff has gone back to *Origin* 1 (Spring 1951), where Olson's essay "The Gate and the Center" appeared.

Ring (The Ring of Minos) and Daedalos really flew in the sky and scorched his wings—and what is more Evans has found the actual tomb and the Aphrodite temple above it described in Diodoros of Sicily as of the last Minos!!

Oh Olson—I am so excited I am going crazy—I am Napoleon with my star burning bright right over my head directly in front of me—after 4 years of agonized blindness I am steering by the surest Radar there is! Talk about fables!

Your Motz

46

Brooklyn to Black Mountain
[26 November 1953]

Thanksgiving

Charles dear—

A very nice black special delivery man brought the exquisite package last night[16]—and I stayed up to read it through—It is now before breakfast and I hasten to tell you, though as you can guess, there is very much which I am not sure of at this first reading, that the primary adjective which comes up to me is clean—that in some marvelous transposition the very air of a Gloucesterman's boat has somehow been made to blow—that the pages are intensely clean and male. That they come to me as *Ishmael* did with a wondrous healing at an hour most needed (I had precisely at five last night a big blow out with my boss). But above all, I want to tell you that this last two weeks I am steeped in Rimbaud's *La Chasse Spirituelle* which I ordered from France and in the light of all that sacred holy thing discloses of Rimbaud's sufferings (I cannot wait to show and talk to you about it) in that high light—where I was touchy and fussy as a priest in his sanctuary—*Maximus* seems the next direct step—it comes over big, Olson—clean as clean—and while it requires, as always, very much hard work on my part to decipher in detail—it has already delivered its message to me and I would say comes out as in absolute, direct succession to La Chasse.

I have found a book which you also must see, "The Sacred Tree Script"[17]—explains things in Rimbaud, in Plato and refers in ways I want to discuss with you to your "Gate and the Center"—very wonderful discovery, to me, and I now think—I can practically draw a literal line of

16 *Maximus Poems 1–10* (Stuttgart: Jonathan Williams, 1953). Boxed edition archived with the Frances Boldereff Papers, Archives and Special Collections, University of Connecticut, Storrs.

17 Andrew Efron, *The Sacred Tree Script: The Esoteric Foundation of Plato's Wisdom* (New Haven: Tuttle, Morehouse, and Taylor, 1941).

exactly how and where the thing has traveled from the beginning of "man's motion"[18]—is not that what you called it?

There were several beautiful things that struck me as I read so hastily—

"In the midst of plenty, walk …"

this whole passage through to the end of this Song is genuine song and I hope will be made a song and sung by someone who feels its music as I do and can hum a tune, as I can not.

It is a strange thing to be a woman—to be as full of your thing you could burst—and yet to have no outlet—I feel my thing growing to a size and a clarity inside me that you'd think it would have to break through in *some* form—yet I can neither sing, compose, write prose or verse, draw, sculpt or any of all those blood passages—perhaps I can squeeze it out into my house, which I am still determined to build before I die!

One other thing—I have an article from the architect Deitrick, on his terrific State Fair Arena at Raleigh, N.C. Most exciting building of the modern world—go to Raleigh if you possibly can—and *see* it—as I plan to whenever I can swing the money—Charles—in that building you will find everything which makes genuine polis—one of the great achievements. And the result of what cooperation and creative joint activity. Please hunt up Engineering News Record—February 5, 1953 an article "Curved Roof on cables spans big arena" and you will thrill to see proof that Gloucester is now in Raleigh, N.C.

Your loving Frances

I only realized a few days ago that the dwarf letter disturbed you[19]—that was not innuendo, Charles—it was straight child—and referred to physical head only—and my remarks, to trying to delve into cause, why, against the obvious, I felt it to be so physically accurate. It all has to do with a play I saw as a child which has become a kind of legend to Lucinda and means something neither of us can convey but which we are clear about, completely, entre nous.

18 "Song 4" of "The Songs of Maximus" has "human motion." The other quotation is from "Song 3."

19 A missing letter. Olson mentions it in his letter of 27 October 1953 (no. 43).

J.S. Dorton Arena, Raleigh, North Carolina, 1952
North Carolina State Archives

47

Black Mountain to Brooklyn (special delivery)
22 December 1953 (postmark 22 December 1953)

tuesday dec 22

Frances:

The enclosed is stupid,[20] but what I would like you to do with it is see that Lucinda has some taste of that pistachio—or "Turkish Delight," as we had it, special—from around the corner, for Christmas. (I remember her disappointment that Christmas back there when … (Actually, no connection: I want her to have this, now!

Yr letter on Thanksgiving was, you'll know, a treasure. And I thought I'd have off to you, by now (for something for yrself) the 3rd book of this year. But it hasn't shown up.[21] And so …

> (Crazy, that '53 was 3 books, no? And the way it is
> now going, (bad sale on Max I) I'm frightened
> Max II is going to have to find another publisher
> (you didn't say if you admired the book-making?)
> But already 54 is looming as a magazine year:
> quarterlies, taking, the stuff. And a new one, maybe,
> coming out of this place …

Frances—

Yr loving
Charles

20 Presumably Olson is sending Christmas dollars.

21 Olson is referring to *Mayan Letters*, the book Robert Creeley was publishing in Majorca. It was delayed in press and later at customs.

48

Brooklyn to Black Mountain
[29 December 1953]

[letterhead: *American Weekly*]

Tuesday

Charles

The Christmas gift was practically magic, I was expecting my family, and Lucinda was counting on a tree—I found myself with one token in my purse when the special arrived and next day I went out and carried home myself (shades of Woodward!) a large tree, higher than my living room ceiling, at least fifteen blocks across Brooklyn and with the money saved from buying in a very humble neighborhood, bought candles, decorations, etc., Lucinda and I having much fun and both terribly grateful that you had the good sense not to take my letter, of the lifting of the ban, too literally. O Charles, it is so true that one must either enlarge or grow smaller. My sister, though personally happier, does not seem to have even the small measure of personal generosity she once had towards me; I sometimes believe that she profoundly dislikes me and with the burning dislike of the small has no use for me in any of my parts, though very ready to worship my child, as though she were an unrelated item, sprung up from "pan spermia."

I want to tell you that Lucinda and I have considerably changed plans for the coming year and I do not want to discuss anything until I am more sure what will happen, but if there is any way at all, I am planning to send her away. Job is to find a school which boards children in a grade so young. Anyway, my job is becoming at last much easier and there begins to infiltrate, urges and ideas and freedoms, which I have long held under and I am going to be one happy woman when I can again give a little creative attention to the personal side of my life my appearance and my surroundings. I am positive it can no longer be withheld from me more than one whole more year. Which also puts me above the attacks of the business world, because where I work, when I work, how many hours, so long as I come up with the dollars demanded is a matter of absolute indifference to me, just to see the job accomplished. And with that freedom of indifference, what a release from the torture of the tyranny and jealousy I have endured ever since I came.

O Charles—I feel like a big sea, spreading out slowly and surely over an ancient peninsula—I have time and large space behind me, and try to oppose the flow!

I have given your Maximus to a very young man in my office, who has been reading it diligently for a month, likes it very much and is now on Ishmael. Somehow pleases me, that anyone with no preparation of any sort as to your way of working or your processes, would desire to jump in and see how far he could swim.

Your Frances

Am longing and so is Lucinda for a visit from you—The printing is so perfect—everything so beautiful, so right, it is exactly as I would have wished to do it myself—so exact, I felt I could say nothing but the one word "exquisite." Mother is here until Saturday—Elizabeth Livingston now lives here—came with her family last Saturday—loved your books and Melville letter.

49

Black Mountain to Brooklyn
13 February 1954

Saturday Feb 13

Frances!

Just this day opened yr letter, & found![22]

My god, how can you forgive me! But have been Mexico, (here for two weeks, maybe less, then back Mex for two weeks AND—I *hope*—then north, and see you![23]

The point is to rush this to cover—haven't even read it, but enough to see it is *all* / the Motz / speech
And the *greatest*, that you up and did it. I shall dig it. And write. O.

This only to
cover
love
Charles

(*Mayan Letters*
still stuck,
customs, Spain)

22 This is a reference to a missing letter. Boldereff had sent him what he refers to in his letter of 20 March 1954 (no. 52) as "your little book." The book was never published, but Olson's gloss of the typescript is reproduced with that letter below.

23 Other than this reference, no Olson trip to Mexico in 1954 is on record.

50

New York to Black Mountain
28 February 1954 (postmark)

Sunday

Charles—

Why don't you hurry up and write to me? I am very very excited because last week a friend gave me some back copies of Architectural Forum and I now *know* that you and I are really sitting in the middle of a terrific great thing—Pretoria, Africa; University City, Mexico; Waikiki Beach, Hawaii; Raleigh, N.C.; Brazoria Co., Texas—these are the places where bloom-bursts of living beauty have already come into existence—oh! Charles, architecture, the great and holy purveyor of man's desire is healing deadness after deadness and is gorgeous as nothing has ever been before—I love all of these answers—all of which I understand minutely—if you will forgive me—they all have Motz printing thinking—little cheap (dollar-wise) ways of turning hum-drum into beauty—all, all, so magnificent. I am not sleeping for three nights—God, how man is bursting his bonds—and on top of this I found last year and now another, two days ago, book of a Russian young theologian of the Russian Greek Orthodox Church—with ideas so Rimbaudian—the church of Russia will give a living religion to the world again—as living as Minoan—for the first time ever last year I found a statement about Original Sin which was tolerable to me in *Apocalypse of History*[24]—

I have been hunting for over an hour and can not find another wonderful sentence I found last night in *Divine Realm*[25]—suffice it to say that the church of Russia is against all narrow and rational people and looks on life as the presence of God here and now—knowing no form of

24 Evgeny Lampert, *The Apocalypse of History: Problems of Providence and Human Destiny* (London: Faber and Faber, 1948).

25 Evgeny Lampert, *The Divine Realm: Towards a Theology of the Sacraments* (London: Faber and Faber, 1944).

life which does not represent a sacrament. In fact I open my eyes wider and wider that the clever language is proving so nicely all of the things I have known and obeyed and could not voice, which were so maligned in the life of the "good" around us.

In New York Public I found some new translations of minor Rimbaud—oh! the closeness and the absolute adorableness of that man.

Write and come

Frances

51

New York to Black Mountain[26]
11 March 1954 (postmark)

Charles,

Terribly disappointed to find the enclosed,[27] instead of a letter, I somehow feel certain it was sent to me on purpose, not by an accident, but why I have no idea.

I saw last night pictures and plans of the house Frank Lloyd Wright built for his son out in the Southwest. It is beauty—unsurpassed. The inside has not been solved by him at all; he has curious things that he loves, such as walls on the inside that look like anything but a home, brick, concrete block and what have you and his fireplaces came out of the stone age. He also designs hideous furniture. I wish he didn't think he was such a hot designer. But the house—the conception, is flowing grace. I am convinced that the great break-up awaited has begun, as good old

26 This letter was readdressed to "c/o Stathes, 2312 Ashmead Pl. N.W., Washington, D.C."

27 By mistake, Olson had sent Boldereff the following letter to his male friend Jean Riboud:

sunday (after
talking to you

jean:

look. I don't believe i will call you thursday. Or leave any message with de Menil. And for the simplest reason: that we have been fantasying & overexpecting this whole deal, of seeing you, & going away, for five months. And it has all gone sour. And the best thing to do is to forget it, clear it away, get rid of it, and then pick up.

SO: you go off and have your trip. And when it is all behind you, and you are squared away without it, in other words when you are free and we are free of it, please then you call us here. And if by any chance we aren't here, Huss will know where we can be reached.

Don't, above all, put any weight on this: it's merely that you cldn't know what a big but terrible winter this has been. And today is the end.

So then, mid-March, somewhere, right?

yrs,

Charles

Spengler says it always begins, in architecture. Not that I accept things like Harrison's church in Connecticut, I consider it tricks and tricks arising out of the supreme mastery of technique, but death-serving.

The pressure on me is maximum from the money standpoint—this time I really do have to move and soon. So by the summer I shall be somewhere else. However, my little daughter is something of a jewel—a gorgeous little mind, being well trained. So it is worth all the torture.

Write as soon as you can.

Frances

52

Brooklyn [written outside 180 Clinton Street]
[20 March 1954]

Friday–Sat
1:45 am

Frances:

Wired you from bus en route. But I guess, not quick enuf! Just on the chance you do come in, I'll stay tonight at the St. George.

Love, Charles

PS The above *was* the letter I *thot* I mailed to you a couple of weeks ago! WOT in the world did I put in that envelope to you?

[Olson wrote the above note by hand on the following typescript, which he meant to send Boldereff earlier]

point is, that the ship is righting itself. And I shall be on to you, instead of this damned silence

actually, i have read and read your little book, and even did a gloss of one half of it for you[28]—

until i figured, hell: this is how frances has it, and she knows what i would, and have, press her to do—a *gloss* of her own, on Rimbaud

or (what i think is finally purer)

her own speech, said out in infinite detail

(it is my old cry, that, if you say

this much you *must* say more—spell it out; or, less: that is, make it wholly your own speech, leaving out all these literary characters!

see you soon

and love,

charles

28 The two typed pages of Olson's gloss are archived at Storrs. Olson seems to be quoting Boldereff's words with some suggested emendations, which he then explains his reasons for.

[Olson's gloss of Boldereff's text]

1. "(The American)—I claim Rimbaud for myself because he and I await the other in a tense awkward circle game of childhood where the winner becomes 'it' and no sooner is in the circle than he runs out, chased, even though just now the 'winner.'"

((*Reasons for changes*: anyone one of us does "choose" or claim a person from the past as much as we do living ones. But it is a greased slide to enlarge such a "claim" by saying "the American" does so choose, simply, that it amounts to a claim not so easily granted: that others make exactly the same "choice." For the mark and distinction is, that each of us make his or her own discrimination. And not one of us can claim exactly what another's is, it is so exact. In any case one persuades another more by allowing the other the chance to agree than any usurpation of sd agreement. The image of the "round" or game has some of the same enlargement if the words are allowed to be unrestricted, and to repeat themselves. They spread as the claim does, and instead of fighting against the intoxication of themselves—words have this weakness—they "let go." And in this instance (of the energy, and "rules", of exactly "Relievo") such letting go, instead of getting the simile, marbelizes the thing like exactly the trouble with the Grecian urn.))

2. "Rimbaud is probably unique as one who had achieved his language and so could speak out despite the confrontation of youth which is, because it is youth and confronted, wordless."

((Here I hope I have the meaning, aware that I am pulling it back from a sounding. Because either it is this remarkable thing, that he could speak so when 15, or it is a point of such density—how it is to be young—that it had better be more said if it is to be worth saying.))

3. "(*American*)—It is a truth, even if a cliché, that *action* is what is most to be remarked as 'American' abt the American; he is accumulating—to break out, not in song, poetry, image, understanding, but in action—action patterned by no name which yet exists, yet it is the woman-man thing of the American, and it will destroy the old allegiances and will follow where Melville led."

((One touches this least, simply, that it is your speech. In fact the only real change is to substitute "thing" for "rhythm", and for the above reasons: that the word rhythm is loaded. And if the woman-man thing is this action, it doesn't need any loading—even another loading I let stand, viz., that such is an action which contradicts song, poetry, image, understanding (as though they weren't "action"!))

4. "Melville wrote his chapter on grandissimus—'*What a lad for a Pope were this mincer!*'—and thereby in language and sentiment quintessential betrayed that America has no intention to be taken off her main beat—that she will doggedly declare for reality."

((I cancel this, for every one of the reasons: (1) Melville wrote abt other things—cf. above, greased slides(!); (2) a writer is his own poor self (!); and (3-n), the clearest meaning of the allusion comes out this: America's main beat—the reality she will doggedly declare for is—a mincer! In other words ... So: if Rimbaud stands to her aid, then he, too ... And the quote from him, if it echoes Blake, makes Blake ... Read this way, then, the tree of good and evil is only buried, and the tyrannical codes are finally Papa's ... oi yoi. Even the very pure love ... Besides, of course, such a beat is hardly America's "own"!

5. "America will follow where Rimbaud leads. He has written the most exact outline." ((How abt giving it?)) "And she will draw the pattern into her ..." ((I excise her "living flesh" simply, that it is not demonstrable that America is a she or has any such thing as ... ((or it is the opposite of ... this country! And as—in essence—no more than as of 1, the only valid statement is: "I will follow where R leads. He has written the most exact outline I know. And I will draw the pattern into my living flesh." (as thruout)

6. "R: I will read aloud for them your orders"—an arrogation conceivable date 1872 but patently—even granting that R was speaking in voice, and that he must be left in that context, not this social exhortation as of these States—questionable, as, applicable, now, 1954

7. "Les mysteres sont morts" (accent grave on first e of mysteres; and the s on the participle is peculiar, in this sense that it strikes me it cld be a plural noun, thus the meaning being, 'The mysteries are deaths'—which is more ambiguous than I believe you read it as, 'The mysteries are dead', no?)

In any case, I don't believe (1) one can speak easily abt same; (2) that you, or anyone, can read same as that mallarkey, "beautiful Greek reverence" (if Blake sd that, he ought to come off it); (3) that three such men as RBD, if they are worth remembering at all, must be because they can't be melted together so presumptuously; & (4) that if we are anything, we are post-modern

and if we are we don't "clunk" anything. In fact, you go on immediately to expose the fact that you don't know what you are talking abt: "enwrapped in the unknown." Which is sloppy as "les mysteres" demonstrably were *not*. Or that fatuity, of Ouspensky, what form, has, the world—my god, MotzBoldereff, if it is a "nice question", it is the question of an idle mind, one which has not itself engaged itself with form. And that's that. It's baloney, to ask, what form, has, the world.

And we damn well are ready with the questions (again, if you sd, I am not yet ready with, you'd be on grounds which anyone can deal with. But don't be so sure that the old questions are to be thrown away, and that there are new questions—this is wordplay, with words, and is of as outrageous an order as playing with any live things—including, human beings.

As you are delighted in your soul—excuse us, please: this land is not given over to death. Or it is, and it is given over to mincers—and not to whatever phallicism that archbishop has been exaggerated to be, an overinterpretation of HM's cuteness over what either better be done straight or not at all

"where even children do not converse with life" (what a conversation that

53

Black Mountain to Brooklyn (special delivery)
7 July 1954 (postmark 7 July 1954)

july 7

frances, my beloved

forgive me forgive me: one week after I saw you in March they made me Rector of this place. It was a push which had to be tried. And it is one of those wild things which would make you pull all the air around you in and roar a Motz roar that though not one cent has yet been added from my efforts, a motor is ready for gas (and Doris Duke will put the gas in, in October!) But the point is that here I am monarch of all I survey! Just the sort of issue you'd appreciate as no one else (in fact you remember Kulikowski, the big rich Pole? well the comedy suggested itself, that i write him saying, i now have 550 acres, a farm of 175 improved acres worth 50,000 dollars, a stock of Herefords larger than his own in Virginia, etc. etc.—just for kicks

For (again you'd get it) I feel so free of it I could close it tomorrow! (Why I did it, and how it is so mobile, is one of those things one will, i suppose, consider and consider—like a Tarot fortune, if it was as good a one as Cagli once read me—for the rest of the life, yes?

i just poured it on, and the one thing i didn't do in the rush was to let you know that that Canadian trip, to read Maximus, was postponed in that same week after (Layton, the poet there, by god, upset me by writing that the Poetry Society had spent all their funds for this year on Viereck, Auden, and Roy Campbell, mind you, and had none left for me! Ho ho. And I still bite whether I will accept the first reading there in October

this is to get off to you the first number of the Review,[29] which, until today, has been tied up in Customs! no less. And not

29 *Black Mountain Review* 1, no. 1 (Spring 1954), printed in Majorca.

for any of those political reasons. Simply that Creeley's wife or somebody forgot to put in an invoice with the shipment. Ditto for *Mayan Letters*—which is still not here, and I shall have to get to you personally

but i ship off the Review: and please, Frances—don't delay a day to let me hear how it sits with you (it makes no sense that this is the first thing of mine out since Max ... except for an angry note in New Mexico Quarterly this spring issue

I still keep thinking of that dream I wrote you from Montevallo.[30] It still feels like a piece of information I would give so much to read again, to see what the hell was going on there. Please (like i gave you back a copy of the great vision—and believe me, tho you slighted it, when you saw it again, it was just such) do, any time you can get your hand into that trunk, haul it out for me. Remember, you can lay your hand on so easily: it will be the one letter sent from Montevallo, Alabama, approximate date, April 30—or make it May FIRST!—1950

Some quiet new poems I'd not yet know the worth of. I had to kick off that Maximus form, in order to do more of it. The vision of the poem is now free-floating in me, in fact out on paper as a conception of itself, of its probable end. But until I explore this simpler sort of thing I shall not want to do any more of that explicit & direct &—elementary?—stuff.

But what you should also know—or I would more tell you,—is, that, I begin to feel the time (which for me would be the locus) is coming when I shall launch the Translations from the Sumerian and the Hittite. And I hunger to be at it. Think of it, Frances: think of it.

Let me at least copy you one of present batch. And to jive, first: this small one

THE INN[31]

Or an inn
up whose leg
her protests
only pleasures
I stand
in the crowd

30 See Olson's letter of 3 May 1950 (*AMC*, no. 213, pp. 328–29) and letter no. 74 (13 April 1956) below.

31 This and the following short poem, "How It Is," have not been previously published.

significant
I am my father

Or another little one:

HOW IT IS

It is there.
Le cri.
Equity,
the man on his stoop,
waiting
for the wrong
to be righted

damn it. can't find a very little poem i wrote as of you many months ago. seems lost! tho i keep my papers in such a state (purposely) that it will turn up. it was very swift. and generalized. and probably of no meaning to anybody but three of us. but it spoke (like, say, that "i am full of blood"). this one was

the copse
where i was
born
where the Beloved

(and it swung off. But i shall find it. and give it to you. it stands, in fact, as a simplification of EPIGON. which was required (?

Well. There is always so much to be done, isn't there, Frances? And here i am pigging the space when what i want to know is what you are up to, how your studies go, if you are all right, if things are in hand, how Lucinda is, how the dream house sits, and of all how you are

how
you
are

Let me hear as soon and as
much as you will

love
yr
Charles

Or why don't I write you a brand new one just like that right here on this page? Yes.

call it—THE REAL[32]

and let it begin thus:

The neck of
the cone, she
on the left, he
all for me, protesting
on the right

did you kiss me there,
she said, pointing

I have a bruise,
she said

You've been funny,
all day

Picasso called it a wound,
I said, not I

And when I got my car out of the mud
it followed me, adhering

32 This poem was unpublished until it appeared in *Collected Poems*, p. 305. Also enclosed with this letter was a typescript of the poem "The Pavement," published in *Origin* 14 (Autumn 1954) and in *Collected Poems*, pp. 301–2.

54

New York to Black Mountain
9 July 1954

July 9, 1954

Charles dear,

Was not home last night when your beautiful magazine arrived and it will be a little while before I can examine it.[33] It is extremely handsome physically. I am glad to note that someone is saying what should be said about Mr. Roethke.

The Sumerian business sounds too wonderful to be true, do you mean translations by Olson? Also I have definitely asked Barnes and Noble to set aside Cornford's *Zeus* $85. for the day when I can beg or borrow the money—you will want to examine it.[34]

I am terribly sorry you did not write to me about a month ago—I was in Woodward for two whole weeks and I just had given you up as lost. The trunk is in a very dark and very hard to get at place in a loft, with another big trunk on top of it and no longer anyone living in the country who specially wants to help me—so I can only tell you I will get it as soon as I can get money to go back. I am still unbelievably without.

We tented for two weeks—two nights of real storms with lightning and hard clashes and terrific wind and rain and Lucinda and I, both naked, hair streaming like a cheap movie, holding on for dear life so the thing wouldn't blow away from us—but wonderful little tent, inside did not even get damp. I had also learned only one night before from my cousin-in-law the GI trick of digging a small ditch immediately around the outside, to drain off excess. Very marvellous how well it works.

33 *Black Mountain Review* 1, no. 1 (Spring 1954).

34 Boldereff is likely thinking of A.B. Cook's multi-volume *Zeus: A Study in Ancient Religion* (Cambridge: The University Press, 1914–1940).

I was utterly exhausted to point of death when I left and the hard uncomfortable earth, with its smells, Olson, restored me, but restored as though I were eighteen. Really gave me back something I haven't had for many years—that terrific feeling of can't miss. Last night I had dinner with Bassett Roberts—first V.P. of National City Bank, a very old friend and he said the thing about you is, Frances, that you have always known you were right. I didn't know how he meant it, but anyway, last night it was right. I came back with that indescribable sensation of the feebleness of the opposition.

I want the Mayan as soon as possible. Lucinda says many times "I like Olson" and there just isn't sense in staying away forever.

I am reading Ischlondsky "Brain and Behavior," real real dope Olson, on how the human operates, tests, intensely interesting.[35] You must see it, I have bought it. I am beginning to believe we are in an era when any art including writing must appear accidentally as a corollary to getting down new knowledge. Maybe you will say that is what you are doing and I could agree, when you really accomplish one, as you say in heat. But it doesn't sound to me as though any of the other writers are—I am beginning to feel very strongly that like the music of the Russians that got written by a variety of occupied men, including the admiral, Moussorgsky, that no man is today permitted to contemplate his navel.

Frances

35 N.E. Ischlondsky, *Brain and Behaviour: Induction As a Fundamental Mechanism of Neuro-psychic Activity* (St. Louis, MO: Mosby, 1949).

55

Raleigh to Brooklyn
12 July 1954 (postmark 12 July 1954)

[letterhead: Hotel Sir Walter Raleigh]

Monday, July 12th

I have seen your State Fair! And wanted to tell you that it is beautiful—will try to see interior as I go back tomorrow (here for a meeting to get Black MT approved to educate Korean Veterans in painting, music, writing, theater, & pottery:

it worked

Drove out of town after meeting to see your building. And what I don't know you'd know from photographs and plans is the force of the lower concrete curve—the one which counterpoints (almost like a frieze) the lovely down-sweep of those two outer roof curves

Crazy thing, is how *symmetrical* the bldg comes off—with that steepness at the maximum vertical of the roof curve (plus the two double knees) actually being—that steepness, & that loveliness of curved wrists—also symmetrical!

Plus the double-cross the roof is—has this "ridge" running from the maximal verticals, & their down-sweep making a ridge roof at right angles to that ridge!

Very beautiful. And delighted you put me on to it.

Also actual, that the old Fair Bldgs are all abt the foot of this lovely feminine thing! Stables etc. Yet it looms, & makes its own space (so much so I spotted it off to the left, first thing I saw in the city.

Well, do write. And tell me if everything is all right with you

All my love,
Charles

56

New York to Black Mountain
15 July 1954 (postmark)

Charles,

I was very happy to have your report on my building—1. because the ribbon around the building is the big reason I love it and it has been an architectural issue lately via Architectural Forum and I have written to Deitrick and received a nice reply about it—2. Elizabeth and Warner drove by recently and saw the building and did not seem to think it was too beautiful—said it did not look attached to the ground—3. I showed the picture to my banker friend and he said it looked like a roller coaster and 4. I have written something as to its feminine nature in my fifty pages on Credo in Unam—would you be interested in seeing it? I am not at all satisfied myself, but there is part of it I think you would like and I may put it out, to sell exclusively to college students, via college newspapers. If you could somehow manage to get it printed in Stuttgart if I could dig up some money, I would surely like to talk over the possibility.

Lucinda is going to Packer next year and everything for next year will be as is. I am wavering since your letter on my other plan, since I think it would be awfully nice if perhaps you and I could work out a scheme to live together a total of some weeks during the year, so that we could have a little more communication.

I walked over the Brooklyn bridge and due to my study of techniques of the roof of the Raleigh building was looking my eyes out at how those cables were fastened on the bridge and that whole thing is so beautiful, my soul simply leaped to behold it. Also it quivers all the time, which both frightens and excites me. I mean all those smaller cables, when you put your hand on them, although visibly they are not moving.

I am delighted about your being Rector and getting the Korean ok and all that.

I have the problem for the whole summer of what to do with Lucinda. Is your cottage in Gloucester rented or sold, and if not, could it be possible for one week, for Lucinda to go there. She has been wonderful but I would love her to have some salt air, and I know someone who would take care of her and cook for her, if it were free anytime before Sept. 22.

I loved your book review[36]—the poem I like and the essay I do not approve of in its manner of writing—the idea is fine, but I do not like the unsilken and rough Olson approach, I think it should be done suavely like Ishmael.

When will it be possible to talk to you?

Frances

36 Boldereff is referring to Olson's contributions to *Black Mountain Review* 1, no. 1 (Spring 1954): a review of *Captain John Smith, His Life and Legend* by Bradford Smith; the poem "On First Looking Out of La Cosa's Eyes"; and the essay "Against Wisdom As Such."

57

Black Mountain to Brooklyn (special delivery)
30 July 1954 (postmark)

Beloved Frances, forgive me, to be so slow to take you up on (1) that you send me pronto the pages on *Credo in Unam*, and (2), to let me have your thought of how, in all this distance and wild time you are, in your way, as wild an inhabitant of as I have been, that you see we might spend more time together! It is crazy, the way you put it—and straight Motz!

But I have been coming down off, and putting myself back in—at least to words. And to do that when still this College gets me, still *deserves* (I take it) what push I can give it that it may live again—and then I shall be free to go forward a more natural way to myself—

But what I wanted to tell you, was this: that my first step in, a month ago, was to try to make *for you* a true translation of—what do you think????—*Credo in Unam* itself!!![37]

In fact, if I had been satisfied, I'd have sent it to you when I last wrote (that is, before Raleigh.

And now I am reading Season in Hell.

It is very beautiful, that, just now—and for the first time, really—I am "free" to read Rimbaud. And this I owe distinctly to you: he was (even when, as John Hines, I did the "True Life" of him, in Key West, 1945) no more than a dark thread I would put my hand on and take it off as (as Theseus) I sought to open up a labyrinth. And only now, say, am I in the darkness. And can see. Or at least gather the thread into my hands.

It takes such *newness*! Oh, Beloved, what newness! I must practice a wholly different self. And my old attentions—my old words—no longer do. It is a shift-over the like of which …

How it is, in the caveless cave! I feel inside out. And walk about with eyes turned out. And look, like a creature who didn't know what is seen now solely as though it was all a revisitation: that is, that I have seen all in

37 The typescript, dated 11 July 1954, archived at Storrs, is quoted in part below.

slices, now I see same as continuous, and in blocks. It is deep and crazy. And all is splendor, even when it isn't.

It is the death of person, I should imagine, the final shredding of that error. And it dies hard: I still ask myself how the conundrum is, that only all you love (and how many there are! and how many loves!) are what make it, and yet that it isn't they, it is life manifesting itself in any one of us—

Je sais aujourdhui saluer la beauté

But all that's the top of the cake. And won't do, for the statement. It's not the what. The how is different. Thus the what is. And one comes back to the man again: Je es.

The translation had some pieces of success:

And in the valley
the earth is nubile, overflows
of blood. The sun's breast
is of love as god is, is of flesh
as woman is, comprehends
the tingling
which all seeds are
…

when man was so,
he was chaste,
and sweet
…

It is a pretty farce,
and the world snickers
at the mention of
Venus

Man is ugly
under the vast
sky. He wears clothes,
he is not chaste, he has dirtied
his own loveliness, he has let shrivel
like a clay piece in a fire his beauty
to low servitudes. He lives
as though he were dead
and in the greenishness

of his own bones. He insults
his own first goodness.

Or this, which you will recognize as an interpolation!

... you will come to him,
all splendor, from the deeps
you will rise, and,
with that mouth of yours breaking
into that wild pleasure (how your mouth is
the face of the depths from which you come, he
came)—the World will be
quivering
from the joy
of the kiss the two of us
will give

o, in the flesh man tests all
—and knows
o splendor
of the flesh, o ideal
splendor, o renewal
of love, triumphal
East

But like I say, American / is not French. We come in from a different angle—even tho it is to the same center. But that angle is not so easily come at.

Well, PLEASE. God, let me see those pages—i can't think of anything I shall eat up as I shall your words!

OH yes. That, most, excuse me. Abt Gloucester, for, Lucinda. But alas: I have no such house. (It was one of the desperatenesses of my mother's death, that I hadn't buried her when Barrett—the man from whom we had rented since 1916!—the day after!—sd, can you get out?! So Con and I stayed there, midwinter, bloody cold, snow etc., and in 48 hrs liquidated a lifetime, burning, giving, hauling, selling all my books, etc. It was the damndest.

Darling, I have no tie left to Gloucester except my poem. And now that, too, has caused such a raucus that I don't even feel free to walk down the Main Street!

If I think of anything else, will be much more quick to tell you.

And will, the moment I can see out, let you know I am coming. But please: write me write me write me write me. Keep em coming. And I shall not lag, now that I am in my own saddle.
All love,
Charles

58

New York to Black Mountain
1 August 1954 (postmark 1 August 1954)

August 1

Charles dear—

Forgive pencil and rush. Am thrilled with your letter. You will not eat up my words on account there aren't so many.

I am mailing the thing to you tomorrow although I no longer want to print it—the only reason I wanted to was to get the wonderful Minoan illustrations out on top of words of Rimbaud—my point would prove itself.

My words are as uneven as possible. Snatches of universal interest, but nevertheless a few lines here and there of some things I have wanted to say for a long time.

I want you to return it and do not please correct it—embarrasses all hell out of me—as though I were a pupil.

It will not be what you want—but I am warming myself up like a pitcher—one of these days I'll be ready to flow.

The translation of verse is my attempt at a literary poem—it is an attempt to be so literal that no little shade of Rimbaud would escape—the beauty and all that I didn't worry about—I just tried to make it the most literal translation possible and above all to keep the words in their exact order—there may be huge things wrong with it since I am far from being a Wallace Fowlie.

I *love* your interpolation—So Olson, so unRimbaud. I think you are too big a man to translate.

Frances

Be not angry with your crazy—I have disregarded the most obvious facts all my life—such as that a shy person like me had nowhere to go to the bathroom for 2 whole weeks while camping—paid high price.

59

New York to Black Mountain (special delivery)
2 August 1954 (postmark)

Charles—

I have a letter I want to write but not time right now.

Love—

Frances

[encl. Boldereff's typescript "Credo in Unam." The typescript contains Olson's occasional marginal notation, often difficult to read.]

CREDO IN UNAM

When Rimbaud said that woman will discover the unknown, he did not at all refer to the work of advancing details of knowledge—in whatever field one could mention—he referred to an act: the act whereby woman works in the arena of the invisible.

The performances of a great man, visible and concrete at the hour of their completion, issue in circles of invisible impregnations; the work of woman, on the contrary, invisible at the moment of its accomplishment, long afterwards results in integrated, visible acts, and at its most effective, fashions a living, distinct being.

It is my opinion that woman has lost her foothold in this hour and that a painful, enormously creative act is obligatory on her part, if she is to regain it.

This book will be an attempt to define what I conceive to be the task of modern woman.

Like the poet Rimbaud, I am enamored of woman at the time of the Minoans. She was then at her best—elegant, graceful, ecstatic and unblundering—as a worshipper of the Great Mother, she embodied in herself the obligations of the intuitive. In order to give some precision to the picture, I have covered the pages throughout with a tissue overlay of Minoan art, so that the feeling of the great extent to which the intuitive has been sullied will overwhelm the reader and place her in a position to comprehend the great cry of Rimbaud's *Credo in Unam*.

Credo in Unam was a notification to the world that the bell was sounding; that the division between the mind of man and the intuition of man was about to be closed; that we could look forward to an era of the intense unification of direct knowledges with informed desires. At this moment there has been constructed on earth a building which I believe to be the symbol "Credo in Unam."

There has never been before on the earth a building which has been a dancer, caught at the instant when she is about to enter a second movement. And this building which is the essence of reverent movement has in its inner appearance, a soothing and exhilarating effect on the individual seated within. Could a symbol be devised which could more clearly worship the true powers of woman? And could any symbol be devised more clearly showing forth the powers of man's mind, the strengths of his coordination, the humility of what he does not know stated in the gorgeous correctness of what he has learned? I believe the name of this building is *Credo in Unam* and the fact that it is a cattle judging pavilion takes us back directly to the Minoans—to their sacred horns where the power incarnate in a bull was translated again and again into art.

Like the Ring of Nestor, Minoan civilization was set down amidst seas, a jewel carven to illustrate the future—a separate, hard, delineation in which is held up before us a life so characterized by the living that it appears to have been worked by God for the education of men when they shall have rid themselves of error and in eye-opening despair are ready to cast about for reality.

Rimbaud, in the depths of his being, was aware of all that today we find elucidated in the magnificent study Arthur Evans has completed for us—a study of such magnificence as to cause a sense of awe in those who fully grasp its unerring intuitions and the breadth of its scholarship.

To anyone who studies one of Rimbaud's earliest poems, Credo in Unam, the feeling is inevitable that in some subplasma beneath the granitic Rimbaud spirituality, there lay embedded a complete fossilized

Minoa—ready for minutest scrutiny in that hardest living object known to man—the eye of Rimbaud.

This poem, written in "the month of love" and sent off in purest and highest desire by its author, sounds like a transcript—taken down, item by item, as a world, turned to intellectuality, cast off one by one the Minoan achievements.

The following quotations are an attempt to bring to the reader some small glimpse of that past achievement—in order to ready ourselves for an understanding of Rimbaud's yearning, his accuracy and his place as a guide in the new world now being born.

[Boldereff interjects eleven typewritten pages transcribed from Arthur Evans's *The Palace of Minos,* volumes 3 and 4, followed by her own typewritten English translation of Rimbaud's poem "Credo in Unam," which she quotes again as the essay proceeds.]

"Credo in Unam" is the finest title to appear in all poetry. It is flung with aristocratic young grace as a blazon across the sky of the world now in birth. What appeared to be only a successful, if neglected, exercise in Parnassian style appears to me as a new testament of instructions in aristocratic new life—a detailed account of those steps by which man is to gain adult stature and I feel that in this one poem is encompassed a vast program for the education of young modern woman.

Since Euripides, no poet has looked with so deep and encompassing glance at the life of woman, as Rimbaud. This young man, whose biographers and exegetes have one and all attributed to him a dislike for, if not disdain and positive hatred of woman, has been the first man since Euripides to see woman's problem with an unprejudiced eye. The immense physical attractiveness of this man who suffered under the blows of desire placed him in a position to be peculiarly alive to and aware of woman's total problem and led him to state his desire for a new woman in a variety of longings.

Credo in Unam means to me, "I believe in wholeness." This wholeness is what the world before Christ knew as chastity and what the Russian still calls chastity. Rimbaud closed his literary life with a statement even more precise: "And I shall be permitted to possess truth in a soul and a body."

In order to understand what Rimbaud means, I think it desirable to look at a passage from William Blake:

"All Bibles or sacred codes have been the causes of the following Errors:

1. That man has two real existing principles: Viz: a Body and a Soul.

2. That energy, called Evil, is alone from the Body and that Reason, called Good, is alone from the Soul.

3. That God will torment man in eternity for following his Energies."

"But the following Contraries to these are True:

1. Man has no Body distinct from his Soul; for that called Body is a portion of Soul discerned by the five Senses, the chief inlets of Soul in this age.

2. Energy is the only Life and is from the Body; and Reason is the bound or outward circumference of Energy.

3. Energy is Eternal Delight."

Credo in Unam is the cry of a man who has been robbed, it is an attempt to erase the moral law of Christianity, to rub off as a dirty oily film the accretions the "good" early Fathers have left to us as their reaction to ancient rites and mysteries.

[Boldereff quotes in full Arthur Rimbaud's poem "The First Communion."]

Burrow says that all modern men are suffering from neurosis. How is it that they are sane in any degree when the incalculable damage wrought by the ugliness of the Church's attitude to the flesh is today pulling down the entire world as we know it?

Credo in Unam is Rimbaud, astride the past and the future, calling to those alive to enter into a new belief, a new way of love—a stricter and more proud thing, where each is unfamiliar and treads the invisible thread of his own line in obedience to the vibrations coming to him across his invisible thread.

What is it that I wish of modern woman and what is the form I should like her to mold herself after? Why am I discontent? Is woman to blame for what she now is and can she improve by returning to the past? My answer is that she can not—that now, woman is being forced for the first time since man began, to come out of her roles—to cease being "Mother" or "Child," not to act any part—for in adult life each adult is an unrepeatable flower—the more adult, the less repeatable—therefore she is being forced to a position where she must suffer, think, then act, i.e., become; each woman a separate God-statement—a passage of life giving off perfume uncopyable.

And so I enter my first charge—what I do not like about woman as she is today.

1. The first and foremost sin of woman now is that she is unable to desire, recognize, or admit the truth about herself. She has no spiritual goal.

[Boldereff quotes in full Arthur Rimbaud's poem "The Sisters of Charity."]

2. The second sin of modern woman is derived from the first—as she seeks not the truth, she has a far higher opinion of her achievements than is warranted.

3. On her great traits, instilled by God, she is losing grip.

RAVINGS I p. 31 "He says: 'I do not love women. Plainly, love must be reinvented. All that women can do is to wish for an assured position. Position once achieved, heart and beauty are set aside. Nothing is left but cold disdain, the food of marriage nowadays. Or else I see women who have the tokens of happiness, of whom I myself might have made comrades, devoured from the first by brutes with the sensibilities of chunks of wood ...'"

4. She is possessive.

5. She neither understands nor believes in man.

6. She neither understands herself nor is willing to pay, to become herself.

7. She is mentally lazy.

8. She is spiritually indifferent.

9. She is physically self-conscious.

10. She is soft.

I proceed to amplify.

Did you ever meet a woman who understood the word "spirit"? Yes ... Well, if woman *can* understand spirit, why does she line up behind the dead? Why is America filled with young women, full of ambition and empty of love? Does a young woman realize that the battle of life is fought out in her life? That every or any minute she sells, she digs a little heap of death around her and in doing so adds to the power of death? A woman has no right to give one little smile insincerely and as for cajoling her way—it is death. Every time a woman is afraid, afraid not to marry, afraid of disdain, afraid of discharge from her employment, afraid to be responsible for her own future, she deepens the heap of death around her. And woman is busy every day avidly selling herself into death. When she extends her bejeweled finger, sign of her Victory, does she see the death she has clasped to her bosom? If woman would dare to act only on love and to suffer the consequences, can you imagine how clean this earth would be—how fresh?!

The sun, the foyer of tenderness and of life
Turns burning love to the ravished earth
And when one is sleeping in the valley one feels
that the earth is waiting and full to painfulness of blood,
that his immense breast, raised up by a soul
Is of love like God, of flesh like a woman
And that he contains, heavy with sap and rays of light
The great swarming of all embryos.[38]

"And following the Phrygians the Athenians, when they initiate at the Eleusinian rites, exhibit to the epoptae the mighty and marvellous and most complete epoptic mystery, an ear of grain reaped in silence. And this ear of grain the Athenians themselves hold to be the great and perfect light that is from that which has no form, as the Hierophant himself, by night at Eleusis, accomplishing by the light of a great flame the great and unutterable mysteries, says and cries in a loud voice, "Holy Brimo has borne a sacred child, Brimos," that is, the mighty has borne the mighty; and holy, he says, is the generation that is spiritual, that is heavenly, that is from above, and mighty is he so engendered." Jane Ellen Harrison, *Prolegomena to the Study of Greek Religion*, Ch. X, p. 549.

How close Rimbaud is to the ancients in their reverence and humility in the presence of the essential mystery, life, can be felt by a sensitive reading of *Credo in Unam*.

And everything believes and all rise up!

38 The beginning of Boldereff's translation of Rimbaud's "Credo in Unam" continued below by more of the translation, interrupted by a passage from Euripides.

O Venus, O Goddess
I regret the time of antique youth
Of lascivious satyrs, of animal fauns
Gods who gnawed with love the bark of branches
And in water-lilies kissed the blond Nymph.

I regret the time where the sap of the world,
the water of the stream, the rose blood of green trees
In the veins of Pan brought forth a universe
When the soil palpitates, green, under the feet of a nanny-goat
Where, kissing softly the clear syrinx, his lips
Entone under the sky the great hymn of love
Where, standing in the midst of the plain he awaits
The response to his call from living nature all around him
Where the mute trees, rocking the bird who sings
The earth rocking man, and all the blue Ocean
And all the animals are loving, are loved in God.

"Will they ever come to me, ever again
"The long, long dances,
"On through the dark till the dim stars wane?
"Shall I feel the dew on my throat and the stream
"Of wind in my hair? Shall our white feet gleam
"In the dim expanses?
"O feet of a Faun to the greenwood fled
"Alone in the grass and the loveliness;
"Leap of the hunted, no more in dread
"Beyond the snares and the deadly press.
"Yet a voice still in the distance sounds,
"A voice and a fear and a haste of hounds,
"O wildly labouring, fiercely fleet,
"Onward yet by river and glen—
"Is it joy or terror ye storm-swift feet?
"To the dear lone lands untroubled of men
"Where no voice sounds, and amid the shadowy green
"The little things of the woodland live unseen."

"There
"Through the appointed hour, they made their prayer
"And worship of the Wand, with one accord
"Of heart, and cry 'Iacchos, Bromios, Lord,

"God of God born!' And all the mountain felt
"And worshipped with them; and the wild things knelt,
"And ramped and gloried, and the wilderness
"Was filled with moving voices and dim stress!"
Euripides, *The Bacchae*, 1.862 and 1.723

Misery! Now he says: I know things
And goes, his eyes closed and his ears closed
And moreover, no more gods, no more gods—Man is king
Man is king! But love, there is the great Faith
O, if man were again to imbibe at thy breast
Great mother of gods and men, Cybele.
If he had not left immortal Astarte
Who formerly, emerging in immense light
In blue waves, flower of flesh that the scented wave
Will exhibit her rose navel where the foam breaks into snow,
And makes to sing, Goddess with the great black vanquishing eyes,
The nightingale in the woods and love in the heart!

O beautiful Rimbaud, lover whom all women would cherish, the only one among modern men to revere as sacred and to surround with holy silence the sacred act of love.

Gardons notre silence
C'est trop beau, c'est trop beau.

(*À Bruxelles*)

And when thou wilt see him sound the entire horizon
Contemptuous of old slaveries, free of all fear,
Thou wilt see him given holy Redemption.

I believe that when Rimbaud said woman would discover the unknown he did not refer to the "unknowns" man has discovered, geographic or intellectual; I believe that he divined that woman would conquer herself in a new kind of warfare and that in her consequent freedom, new possibilities would arise both for herself alone, for the "unknowns" between man and woman and thus, by extension, for man alone. "Redemption."

I search history for as far back as I am able to find records, I find no hint in it anywhere that woman has ceased to regard the mundane shell as important, has looked upon her flesh as enslavement and has realized that in order to emerge from her cocoon she must attack the enemy where it lives—within her.

When free love has been the vogue, apparently all that happened was that one kind of tie was exchanged for another—the few couples whom I have seen living together in free love were more hopelessly tied down than any married couples I know. The woman—far from seeking freedom—was extracting the most absolute kind of devotion and attachment from her lover as though he had to "pay" for her loss of legal status by a heightening of his ties. This is all absurdity.

Woman must expand her horizon—fight with herself daily and hourly until she is capable of loving a man with all her heart and soul and of permitting to him at the same time all free exchange, mental, spiritual and physical with as many other women as he can find who inspire him. It is certain that man has been dreaming of this for a long time, but woman has never seen that the task of cutting this knot was hers.

That such freedom would at once destroy a huge block of ugly suffering in the universe is obvious. But think what it would do for children! If woman, acting large, were herself to command herself absolutely, so that the contemplation of her lover's ecstasy in another woman's arms would fill her soul with a deep "I believe"—think how large and free her bringing up of children would be—the lack of ugly angers she perpetually is guilty of—today to a degree verging on the hysterical.

As I walk through this city I see every day silent little scenes between mother and children which cause the heart anguish. The guiltless child is yanked, screamed at—shaken—abandoned—made to feel guilty—trace back the cause—a mother, profoundly dissatisfied with her own slavery.

Women have lacked courage to attack themselves. Their enemy is their attempt to hold. When the day comes that woman does not attempt to hold any man's love—but is strong to receive what is given, woman will become a true mother and mankind can move forward into a more adult search.

And these awakenings, fresh, clear, laughing,
towards the adventure
Of the proud damned with a most magnificent sabbath
And salvation, witness pure of the soul in this combat
For the freeing from heavy nature!

(*The Passions*)

The woman I see is the woman Rimbaud saw …

She will make the suffering of the present seem as nothing in the glory of her being in existence.

Freighted with an intimacy known in Minoan times, she will so intensely encompass the reality in the thousand kinds of life around her that she will no longer know the temptation to death. Woman, alive in her every corpuscle, will move from inner knowledge. She will not seek to imitate man's worship—kneelings will be past—woman will conceive and consult within herself every day an image carved out of her own suffering.

I want her to walk *beside* man—to assign herself a task and accomplish it. I want her to run ahead of Rimbaud's Genie and await with laughter his walking by her side. She is to be neither ahead nor behind nor enclosed of man. She is to touch on reality where it is and every moment in all her dealings. I want a woman and a man to be joined as fire is joined with flame.

"O my good! O my beauty! Atrocious fanfare where I do not tremble. Fairy rack! Hurrah for miraculous work and for the marvellous body, for the first time! It began with the laughter of children, it will end with them. This poison will still be in our veins even when the fanfare dies away and we have to come back to the old inharmonious surroundings. O now, we so worthy of these tortures, let us fervently gather in that superhuman promise made to our body and our created soul! This promise, this madness. Elegance, wisdom, violence! The promise has been made to us to bury in the shade the tree of good and evil and deport tyrannical codes of honesty, so that we may bring forward our very pure love. It began with certain distastes and ended—not being able to seize on the spot this eternity—it ended with a riot of perfumes.

"Laughter of children, discretion of slaves, austerity of virgins, horror of figures and objects from this place, holy be thou by the memory of that night. It began with the awkwardness of a country bumpkin and it came to an end with angels of fire and ice.

"Brief night of intoxication, holy night! even if it was only for the mask you bequeathed to me. We affirm thee, method. We will not forget that you have glorified yesterday each of our ages. We have faith in that poison. We know how to give our life in its entirely every day.

"Now is the time of the Assassins."

Every woman should read this passage reverently. It is the most perfect tribute that has ever been paid to the power of the passions, when exchanged, to illuminate and strengthen the life of man. We owe Rimbaud, as we owe De Quincey and Francis Thompson, to a woman who knew how to give love and was there at the moment it was sorely required.

Rimbaud was physically a stronger man than De Quincey and Thompson and the love he received was physical—but that at this moment in his life he came into the hands of a real woman, experienced and with the great heart of a mother (the opposite of sentimental), who knew how to turn his lack of experience, shyness and ineptness into beauty—we can have no doubt. The proud powerful man who emerged from this night—able to accomplish a life of the sternest holding fast that has ever been achieved was made a man by a woman, by that method, as he rightly says, which has glorified every great age in the past.

He calls it poison, and he is right, for love travels through the veins with the speed of lightning and sets us down on the far side, a victim to its dazzling allure, are we not ever so wary.

Holy, holy, holy is the drunkenness of Dionysus.

But on the day that one seeks to capture this ecstasy, to pin it fast, to make it domestic—the life of man goes sour.

And this is where the lecture begins.

Young women, Rimbaud said, "it is the beloved, not tormenting not tormented. The beloved."

Have you checked yourselves each day, at the close of the night, to ask yourselves—"Did I torment?" Only a woman alive can refrain from tormenting. Only a woman with a goal which is at all times pressing her is able to relate to a man freely. Is there a single one in all America who has no ego, who neither torments nor is tormented?

Dostoyevsky said, "So unfamiliar with life have we become that at times we feel for reality a positive loathing and can not bear to have it brought to our notice. Indeed, so far have we advanced as to look upon real life almost as a burden, a term of servitude, and to agree that the better course is to live strictly in the bookish manner. But why do we also, at times, grow restless, captious and querulous? Even you do not know the reason. Yet if our querulous petitions were to be granted we should find ourselves in a far worse plight. For suppose we were given complete independence, and freedom to bestow our love where we willed, and a wider sphere of activity and increased exemption from tutelage. Why, I assure you that we should very soon be asking to be taken in hand again!

"We do not even know where present-day reality is to be found, nor what it is called. Whenever we are left to our own devices, and deprived of our bookish rules, we at once grow confused, and lose our way—we know not what to do, nor what to observe, nor what to love, nor what to hate, nor what to respect, nor what to despise. We grow weary of being human beings at all—of possessing real, individual flesh and blood. We are ashamed of being human—we account it beneath our dignity. Rather we aim at becoming personalities of a general, a fictitious type. Yes, all of us are still-born creatures, not children sprung of living fathers; and that fact is coming more and more to please us. Soon we shall have invented a way of being born of nothing but ideas."

A long time ago it came to me that fear is lack of love. There simply is not imaginable any situation which properly speaking should arouse fear. Fear is putting a word-in-the-mind in the place of a reality; it is the absence of understanding and it is so completely possible to walk around the earth without fear that it is laughable to realize how man makes such a bug-a-boo of fear. Out of vanity and ego—mother seeing herself so full of love and caring—instead of living and letting her child live.

Which is not at all to imply there is no such thing as evil, nor to imply that one should not recognize one's enemies. Rimbaud says, "However, the corpses of the wicked and slothful fall on the heart of others."

I wonder how many people notice that wicked and slothful are the same thing. Slothful has nothing to do with business affairs; its opposite is not American activity. Slothful is to pounce on the hopes and achievements of the alive and strangle them—slothful is to make fun of the physically graceful because we are not one of them—slothful is to let the mind doze, repeating dead, very dead stupidities and loving it, calling it "goodness," "reliability," "steadfastness," etc. There are not five great big people with pure open hearts in the whole of this country.
D.H. Lawrence preached that we should place big men before us—but he made fun of all the big men he talked about.

D.H. Lawrence wanted the same wholeness that Rimbaud did; they both understood that the pagan "touch" had gone out of our world; the enormous difference is that D.H. Lawrence was sick and envious and Rimbaud was perhaps the finest lover among all white men since Christ—

Rimbaud had "touch," so that Ras Makonnen said he had lost his soul when he heard that Rimbaud had died. Everywhere he went he was at home. He was at home with a dog, or a grass hut or a beautiful woman or an idea. He held nations and their relationships in his fingers the way Jeanne D'Arc did—the instinct, unerring, of a being alive.

Why do the living beings of this earth take the only life they will ever have and do their best to destroy it? Almost everything they can not have is denied them because they choose to be dead. Lord, I have often wondered in my heart why they want to be so poor, when the riches is uncountable right in their fingers. Why do they desire harm to me because against their will they love me because I am alive and at every single opportunity given, they choose over and over again, death?

Why in the name of God women want to wear a beautiful satin evening gown and appear splendid at the price of going home to pretend to caress a man who is putrid, when the world is full of men who know how to clothe a woman in the satin of rhythm is a fancy question.

No wonder Christ said on the cross, "Forgive them Lord, for they know not what they do."

I declare war on the dead.

I despise them.

I will give them not one evening's pity.

I am their enemy and I am out to see them conquered. They have held this world in their power long enough. Let us return to the Minoan harvest singer on the rhyton and be as he is.

And woman can be the one to bring about this victory. Let woman learn to relate herself to a man in a living way. Let her never never give any excuse whatsoever for choosing to live one day, a year or a lifetime with a man whose body is not one with hers. Let her use her mind to guide her in her tasks. Let her seek not the admiration of others, but the inner knowledge that she has obeyed what her own reality requires of her. It is a funny funny thing but God bears the brave on his shoulders just as the pictures of St. Christopher show.

We are in a moving, interweaving world where everything is made of something and there isn't any way yet to describe how the something visible to us (microscope or not) differs from the something invisible, the visible being as deep a mystery as the invisible. But we *know* that the power of a living man is impossible to be covered. The depth of a man's living is registered *exactly* in the frightening (because so accurate) human eye. Therefore, let woman study earnestly her own depths and every eye will be fathomable.

Rimbaud said, "Would Charity be for me the sister of death?" Let every mother ponder this question in her heart. The mother of Christ as shown by the great Michelangelo is great because in her heart she allowed him to be crucified. The distance lying between the mother and the son in the Pieta at St. Peter's is all the distance there is in the world. It is the distance of absolute freedom which is the new command and guerdon of love.

I, who love you, do not dare inwardly to approach the sanctity of your inviolable reality—I am not permitted to save, pity, plead or suffer. I dare only to comprehend. I look, I see. You reach into my seeing and carry your member bravely. This mighty ocean of powerful belief—this lies as the matter of the new lover's universe. On this ocean the raft of each is sailed.

And when Rimbaud speaks of the altar of the flesh, he means exactly what he says … did that great man Michelangelo make himself clear to you … or did he labour and ye still are blind?

I have never ceased to give thanks to God that He keeps the laws of life in His own hands. If a man obeys the living he can not be put to death nor robbed of posterity—his life and his children spring up everywhere; and a woman can no longer count herself among the mothers until her children be voted to her out of life, her living deeds.

It is a proud thing that a man is assigned a task by God. When I think of Blake, writing at fourteen, a poem which was perfect and which announced his later themes, when I read *Credo in Unam* and realize that in this poem lies implicit all of Rimbaud's suffering—his goal and his contribution, I feel certain now, as I knew when a child, that God assigns tasks where He will, that age has absolutely nothing to do with recognition of one's task.

And I now feel that in a certain physical way, the manner of which we do not yet know enough to understand, in my youth I had contact with Rimbaud. When I was quite young, for a long time the same image kept recurring to me … I saw myself, seated on a curbstone in a large city, an ancient ugly hag … I had breasts absolutely flat and hanging down with the tip lying flat against the flesh. I had skin of an unpleasant brownish gray … I had warts and hairs on my face and in my ears, my head was dirty, greasy and thin gray … my hands were claw-like and my clothes were mere covering—and in my eyes the love of truth. And every day I saw myself thus and longed that some one should come and look into my eyes—how many times, over what years I had this image I do not remember, but I recall as though at this moment it were happening that once, someone leaned towards me from above, someone who had no body and no features—and all I saw were his eyes, and they looked *into* mine. From the day that happened I have never seen this image again.

Since I have made such a deep study of Rimbaud, and since I feel that every moment of his life, of the actual dropping of his blood from one height into another passage of his body is known to me in immediate knowledge—since every word, gesture, suffering, decision and attitude is known to me as deeply as I know myself, maybe better, I have come to believe it is possible, though I have the kind of pride which would despise trying to convince anyone else it were so, that the eyes which looked into mine, were his. Whether this is so or not is of no moment, since I and he are related in a profound blood tie, far deeper than any I have ever heard of.

I do not derive comfort from this in any sense; on the contrary, the pain and suffering in his life sometimes almost stops my breathing, nor am I able to believe that either of us is able to gain anything from the other in rapprochement—he went his way alone—I go my way alone—Melville said, "We are the crumbs Christ breaks at his Communion." And each is separate. But I believe I continue in my life a part of the work he began—my part, the part assigned to me.

The theme of my task is from St. John (The Revelation of St. John the Divine, Chapter XXII).

"And I John saw these things and heard them. And when I had heard and seen, I fell down to worship before the feet of the angel which shewed me these things. Then saith he unto me, *See thou do it not*: for I am thy fellow servant, and of thy brethren the prophets and of them which keep the sayings of this book: *Worship God*."

60

Black Mountain to Brooklyn
9 August 1954 (postmark)

o Frances!

You & Rimbaud,[39]
you are right to love the Great Mother,

and to despair in a time when Kore only
(when Demeter has to be looked for)

when only the Maiden (when woman
does not know she is also who hunts
for herself ...
instead of finding half herself
in every ad.

There is no hell when hell is
toothpaste. And Demeter

Oh, Woman:

39 This poem, with the title "I Believe in You ...," was published in *CIV/n* 6 (1953) and in *Collected Poems*, pp. 306–7.

lay about you!

Slay!

that you may have cause again

to seek yourself, to go out among flowers crying

"Kore! Kore!" (knowing

the King of Hell

also has you

love,
Charles: merely
a 1st note

61

New York to Black Mountain
11 August 1954 (postmark 11 August 1954)

August 11, 1954

Charles dear,

Thanks heaps for the poem—it expresses very neatly and very Olsony one of the things that is disturbing me. Makes me feel happy that you so completely understand—everyone else seems to get only one tiny angle and miss the whole.

I have been wanting to tell you apropos "Je suis un autre"—it flashed across my mind the other day as I was looking at it in context that the meaning of this phrase is not at all what the exegetes have explained it to be. It is a very literal statement which does not apply to Rimbaud personally. It means, the I of me is something other than myself. He uses the phrase twice; twice he spells Je with a capital. I am positive that this is a statement of philosophic content, expressing the truth which you were feeling for in your letter "that I have seen all in slices, now I see same as continuous."[40]

I am going to copy out some words I wrote in my first little notebook when I was in my middle teens. I believe the meaning to be exactly what Rimbaud is talking about. "It is so altogether right and joyous that the best of us is what we can not help. The beautiful in us that others love, all we have desirable, is far above us, not responsible to us. God did make it; loves it, nourishes it. What I love about another is not that which he willfully does to please me or does in answer to some hidden sense of 'ought,' but just the perfection in him, created, indestructible."

40 Boldereff is referring to Olson's letter of 30 July 1954 (no. 57).

Lucinda is here with me now in my office, Charles, we are maybe going up to Woodward this weekend; she is so very lonesome here. When we do go, I shall try very hard to find the letter with the dream.

I can not write more now, except to say that you can not imagine how happy it makes me that you are reading my man.

Great love,

Frances

Part Four

1 OCTOBER 1954–26 OCTOBER 1955

The "unconscionable life" Olson refers to in the first letter of this section is his current situation at Black Mountain where both Connie and Betty are resident. Boldereff responds to the man who has been "rescued into Life" (no. 64, 20 November 1954), but the fact that she immediately invites him to Thanksgiving dinner shows how evasive Olson's letter has managed to be. In her 27 January 1955 letter (no. 69) Boldereff finally has to say that she is "very disturbed" about him. Olson's reply (no. 70, 17 February 1955) is a rather stonewalling performance. He is not saying what must be foremost in his mind, that Betty is six months pregnant. The stonewalling apparently continues for some time in silence or in letters now missing.

RM

Black Mountain College, North Carolina, period postcard
Western Regional Archives, State Archives of North Carolina

62

Black Mountain to Brooklyn
1 October 1954 (postmark 2 October 1954)

oct 1

frances—

i live an unconscionable life these days. And you must forgive me anew, & again, & altogether too often & too long for leaving out the touch of connections—

not one whit less of the love was born five years ago, & my utter belief in you, in you in my own vision, my great Lady

i have this sense, that I have left the shores of privilege, & am for the first time swept into the currents of life (following you, in that sense

and it is all so unknown to me (i am life's neophyte, at 43 thrown from naivete into a fragile opening innocence you, I take it, asked of my eyes (talking, of Carl Olsen's, son!)

it all seems dreadfully delayed, that a man shld be so late to come to grips

yet I can do no more than take it it is how I had to be—(& it is not the least consolation that you, in your wisdom, allowed me 10 years!!

Oh Frances there is so much to do, isn't there? And yet one does grow old, and this is the pity of it (even if I feel young now in the proper sense almost for the first time!

In short, a love letter.

(this news, too—that my "poem" to you on yr mss. (which I took the liberty of entitling *I believe in one*[1] ((thus, I hope, not stealing in any way from yr own important fetish, UNAM)) (((it moves me to use the accusative, as I dare say you are moved that he did!))) is already *published!*

1 The published title is "I Believe in You ..."

In Canada (which also seems very damn right. For these Canadians these days are beautiful—& I don't mean yr Northrop Frye, in fact the very poet, say, Layton, whom Frye, in print, has missed the point of! As soon as I get a copy you shall have the issue (CIVn, is its name, Poundese for Civilization) it still rings, the poem, as one with the true, *changes!*

Well, a note this morning of the true life

fr yr lover,
Charles

63

New York to Black Mountain (special delivery)
4 October 1954 (postmark 5 October 1954)

October 4, 1954

Charles dear,

Odd thing. I have been talking to you constantly for the past several days—while your letter was on its way to me. And it is so typical of a mother's life that this letter with its news the most important in the world was found by me as a kind of accident under a heap of piled up school books, notebooks, loose paper, pocket books, etc. of a sub teen-ager! No mention by my offspring—just some electricity that made my finger go over and pluck it out.

I am very quiet with your news—it is the most important thing you could possibly have told me—I have come to a practically violent hatred of everyone in the modern world who is not directly and sufferingly encoiled in the meshes—everyone else is dead. I despise all fortunate (so called) people because today is a day when any man who is alive must be at enmity with the world around—must be poor—must be directly engaged with the monster—never call Northrop Frye "my man"—I never answered his last quite flattering note because he made no response to your poems which I sent him as a gift—so I decided he was a dumbbell. I still continue to study him assiduously because he is a former theologian and he knows the actual meaning of all those names and things in Blake—I am coming to consider Blake one of the biggest *minds* that ever lived. I am beginning to get the complete story à la Blake of the world's origin destiny etc and he is so sound I can not find any loopholes—

I am slowly approaching the complete understanding of my own job.

Also I am coming to love Melville *very* deeply. I am seeing him not at all as he was in his sour old age but as he was as a man before they succeeded to de-sex him. I am reading *Typee* and I love every word of it—the English edition with the most beautiful passages on the dance, etc.

I have had very grave goings on in my own house—due to having no money it has been several years since either L. or myself has gone to a dentist. She had an abscessed tooth—four others in very bad condition and the day after the tooth was drained she got an infected knee which paralyzed her—and she had three bottles of stuff as thick as bees' wax tapped from her knee cap—full of poison—has been in bed for some weeks and is now I hope getting better, although she said tonight it hurt her a lot.

I have teeth in even worse condition and there are large pads of poison traveling around which I can see and feel—on my hands, face and one leg—although I do not look ugly—it is not at all like pimples—it is huge soft pads of flesh—itchy and sore—which shift from place to place—and I have had to listen to 3 lectures from the dentist—several others from doctors, etc—when it is a miracle that I am alive.

My family are nice but stupid—

Yesterday or the day before I saw the marvelous performance of *Midsummer Night's Dream*—God—what a deep play—Olson—deep, deep and understood by one Frances in an immense clarification, after studying Blake so hard—God—I see all of it—what it means—one of the deepest plays ever—I was so moved I sat grinding my teeth—could hardly stand the pressure in my blood of the terrible emotion it aroused—the living power of the living—straight from Shakespeare to Motz.

Olson baby—good that you are recovered from the dead—great good thing—you have taken on yourself a bit of exercise—like you say—but I am 100% on your side and will aid you in any way within my power.

If you get that Yucatan stuff in shape that you wanted somebody to give you a fellowship to work on—why not send to the editor—I will give you his home address—if you wish—I sent your Melville to him and I am afraid some dog has stolen the book and the letter as he is still very cordial but has never mentioned it—

Pray to the Irish saints to let my poison drip on the stones of death in this city—

Frances

64

New York to Black Mountain
[20 November 1954]

Saturday night

Charles dear—

Your letter gave me great happiness—for a long time after I received it I kept being happy and not knowing why—and then I remembered—oh yes! Charles—you can not imagine what pleasure I have in the thought you are young—alive and unhappy—as darling Blake says,

> Joy and Woe are woven fine
> A clothing for the Soul Divine

I am thrilled to my toe-tips that a man has been rescued into Life.

I am wondering if you possibly could buy or steal your way here for Thanksgiving. I was planning to go to Chinatown, and much as I hate to cook—if you could come—I would rustle up some food and we could "give thanks" together.

Had a note this morning from Jay Leyda—he sends you his greetings—asks me to give you his new address—which I believe is 91 Pineapple St.—Bklyn.

Try and come sometime soon—you won't have to spend any money while here—it would be fun for you and me to entertain Leyda and his wife.

I did not realize the poem was for me—oh! Olson—it was always meant that you were to weave my words for me—wasn't it? Answer soon—

Frances

65

Woodward to Washington
[21 November 1954]

Sunday morning

Charles dear—

I can only say I am aghast at what a master I am of the infelicitous phrase. The letter I sent you last night, to correct any wrong impression my first answer may have created was even worse—

But I always count on your understanding because it has always been so miraculous—the decision you have made is the most active one imaginable—but since I am *very* deep in Blake I am moving around in a place where the action of the "*Eternals*" is so present that I can use a word like "rescued" meaning something very different from what anyone would mean—
the great power of a lovely boat to come through a storm eighteen times its size (just in its immediate surrounding area) and vast beyond that.

And this is only to say Charles that I am thrilled beyond all measure—the phrase of "a bit of exercise" in my first letter was the wry face I am making over my own memories over the past few years of the agony it costs just to keep bread in one's mouth—if one intends not to sell any gifts to the devil.[2]

This house is so lovely on Sunday mornings—we now have a new bedroom—you can have the big bed for your own comfort.

I am really reading Blake these days—and coming across many things I have not seen before—if you want to make another wonderful book—
I have a long list—starting with "Portrait of the Artist as a Young Man"—
of places where Joyce has quoted Blake or made immediate direct references to him—and I am sure the key to *Finnegans Wake* is in the organization and form and basic symbolism of Blake's *Four Zoas* and

2 Boldereff is referring to her letter of 4 October 1954 (no. 63).

Jerusalem—I wish I had the kind of mind to trace this out—but having once jumped at it, I am practically through—However, I am deeply convinced that Blake was the brother or father of Joyce in the sense you described of Lorca to Whitman. And much much more—because all of Blake's basic concept of how this world was formed has been taken over by Joyce—and literary devices even to beginning with a sentence which was the last sentence of a previous poem.

Please come as soon as you possibly can. Lucinda wants you, too.

Frances

66

New York to Black Mountain
7 December 1954 (postmark)

[letterhead: *American Weekly*]

Charles dear,

I walked up the street with Heyn the other night and he said your book had never reached him and that he would like to read it, as soon as he can find it. They are searching.

I saw Leyda the other evening and he asked me to ask you if you would be kind enough to lend him your copy of *Eisenstein*. He needs it for some research he is doing and does not have enough money to buy it. I think if you are kind enough it would save lots of trouble to mail it to him directly to 91 Pineapple St., Brooklyn 1.

Every day I am hoping to receive CIVN. I am wondering what and where you are in regard to those Mayan letters. Did this ever arrive and will I ever get to see it? Lucinda is probably your most loyal fan in the U.S. and is always asking where you are. And very effectively dampens any intentions to go off in matrimony or other foolishness on my part.

I am extremely anxious to know how things are with you. I take it for the present the only thing you can do is to stay where you are. How much time does this leave you and how do you feel about being there?

Things are going better with me and I am feeling good. I am definitely going to try to tick off a small very small place at Woodward if possible before 1955 is up. That would give me table room somewhere where I can think.

It is very not kind of you to not to write at all and Leyda says he feels very badly about never hearing from you.

You probably get furious—but be unfurious and write.

—Frances

[Olson has written the following lines on the envelope, although it is not clear if they are in any way related to the letter enclosed.]

A woman wants all of everything
& if a man gets caught in front of that snowplow

A woman wants all a man
A man's
got more to give!

67

Black Mountain to Brooklyn (telegram)
24 December 1954

MRS FRANCES BOLDEREFF
180 CLINTON ST
ALL GREETINGS YOU BOTH YOU WONT BELIEVE THIS BUT CANADIAN MAGAZINE ONLY CAME YESTERDAY WILL SEND[3]
LOVE
CHARLES BLACK MOUNTAIN COLLEGE

3 *CIV/n* 6 (1953) containing Olson's poem "I Believe in You" was sent to Boldereff, inscribed "UNAM Charles."

68

Black Mountain to Brooklyn
17 January 1955 (postmark 18 January 1955)

[letterhead: Black Mountain College]

Jan 17/55

Frances: You must damn well be sore. And you have a right to be. For I sure should have got the Eisenstein off to you. And do, in this mail.[4] And hope it is not too late for any good that Jay may have needed it for. And please forgive me (let me shoot in the enclosed for what it may hint of what one might be up against just at this time of year in this place. It always happens, and yet one hasn't been the wiser. I haven't, the twice now. But get wiser: that just when you think you'll be free, when, in fact, you are supposed to be, this is the winter break, one is off, like they say, only no, not if you have any of the try to make it a place where ... I could spit.

Miss hearing from you. And hope to see you soon.

Love, Charles

Black Mt Review #4 just in & will include—oh, no, what am I talking abt—it's the air mail copy for the characters here!

[encl. flyer "To All Those Who Care for Black Mountain College and What It Has Stood for, and Now More Than Ever Stands for, in American Education," 15 December 1954]

4 Marie Seton's *Sergei M. Eisenstein* (New York: A.A. Wyn, n.d.) was later returned to him and is part of his library.

Black Mountain, North Carolina
December 15, 1954

TO ALL THOSE WHO CARE FOR BLACK MOUNTAIN COLLEGE AND WHAT IT HAS STOOD FOR, AND NOW MORE THAN EVER STANDS FOR, IN AMERICAN EDUCATION:

This is the craziest sort of appeal. Here we are all the way out as a new College, reconstituted a year ago, thriving, as we shall describe it for you below, land & buildings intact, new faculty, new students, and a new Advisory Council—

And yet, if you yourself don't answer this appeal almost as soon as you get it, if funds of a proportion fit to meet the budget outlined below (and please note that it is a 3-year budget, giving a sign of how determined we are to push forward what has gone so marvelously forward in the past year)—

if these funds we are asking of you are not forthcoming, we will be forced to sell part at least of the land, or to take other equally drastic steps.

We have done our utmost, and can show results. But financially we are in distress which only help from any and all friends, supporters, believers, ex-Black Mountain people, unknown people, anyone, can now pour in. We need support now, right now, so much so that we are setting a date inside of which the success of this drive will have to be measured:

on receiving this, and at least before January 15th, let us have all you can give. And all you can pledge.

We appeal to you. But let it be clear, right from the start: the College has changed. A year ago September those of us who are the nucleus of the present faculty refounded the College. And for a year have hired, contracted, devised, sought with all our wits to give the place the lift called for, in the 1950s.

We announce to you, first, a new Advisory Council: Albert Einstein, physicist, the Institute of Advanced Studies, Princeton (whose statement on behalf of the College we attach to this appeal); Franz Kline, painter, New York City (whose presence on this Council makes evident that Black Mountain's long record in painting is intact, and forward with the new College); Carl O. Sauer, geographer, head of the Dept. of Geography, University of California (who stands to us as the figure of the new sciences of man discussed below); Norbert Wiener, mathematician, Massachusetts Institute of Technology (who signs this appeal, along with the new Rector); and William Carlos Williams, doctor, Rutherford, N.J., and chief American poet (who speaks for the new writing and publishing developments of the College).

The Faculty has been this college, and you will want next to know who are the present members you would be supporting. They are: in painting, Joseph Fiore; in music, Stefan Wolpe; in theater, Wesley Huss; in weaving, Tony Landreau; in writing, Robert Creeley and Charles Olson; in languages, Robert Hellman; in pottery, J.B. Blunk (expected from Japan, June, 1955); and in the new science of man, Martin Sprengling, formerly of the Oriental Institute, University of Chicago (invited, Spring Quarter, 1955).

Another major change is in fee: any student can now get the full college calendar year (33 weeks, room, board and tuition) for the same fee that veterans under the Korean or second GI Bill are able to come here, approved as the College is, for education under the new bill, in painting, music, writing, pottery: $850 is the total charge.

We are able to offer education at this rate because of another change: a year ago the College contracted itself to order its buildings and its finance in line with its smallness. Which is what this subscription appeal is about. We can now operate on a budget of less than $25,000 a year. And we propose, by writing to you, to ask you to do your part in making up that amount along with everyone else: with the students who pay an $850 fee, with the faculty which takes no salary but gets a food allowance per month, and with friends of the College who subscribe larger amounts.

We imagine there is one thing more you deserve to know: what change, if any, there has been in the stated purposes of the College. So far as we can see, no essential one. That is, the ownership stays the same: the Faculty is the Corporation. There is the same student-faculty life here. And the arts are meant to be no more than they were in the founding: to share the center of the curriculum with the more usual studies.

Beyond that, one can say this: education in the 50's and 60's ahead, if it is to do what Black Mountain did for the 30's and 40's, involves just such a change forward as we have made in the last year:

1. It has to be cheaper. And that we've done.

2. It has to be, we take it, more centered on the arts. To take, as one example: in writing in the past year the College has added a new

international quarterly, *The Black Mountain Review*; the Divers Press is under the wing of the faculty in writing; and the Jargon Press has its "home" here.

3. And it has to intensify two disciplines which the College has found more and more to be the crucial disciplines to be side by side with the arts and language: exact science (why we carry Einstein and Wiener so naturally on our Advisory Council); and what has to come to be called the "new sciences of man," anthropology, psychology, mythology, the geo- and bio-sciences (we are proud to have Sauer on our Council to advise us in those fields, and the addition of Martin Sprengling to the faculty this spring serves to take a step further what the Institute we held in those sciences in 1953 did to or former practice.)

This, then, is a quick summary of Black Mountain College, 1955. It is new, it is forward, and it needs your help. We have to have money at once to meet this year's budget. There is no illusion possible, no delay, no acquiescence. We ask you to give all you can immediately to meet 1955's $25,000 costs, and to pledge what you can for the next two years as well. A $25,000 budget is one inside which the contribution of any of us, however small, can count: give a dollar, if you can't give a thousand! Please fill out and return the attached pledge. And do it up to the limit of your capacity. Make all checks and pledges payable to:

The Treasurer
Black Mountain College
Black Mountain, N.C.

Our greetings, and our thanks.

For the College,
Charles Olson, Rector.

And for the Advisory Council
Norbert Wiener

The Treasurer
Black Mountain College
Black Mountain, N.C.

I enclose $ _________ as my contribution to this year's budget; and
I subscribe $ __________ for each of two additional years

____

____

January 16, 1954

To whom it may concern:

I have followed since years with a vivid interest the development of Black Mountain College. The reason for this interest is that I am convinced that education without a vivid personal relationship between all working together there, students as well as teachers, is far from the ideal even if the teachers are of the highest standing. The University has not only to transmit knowledge from one generation to the other but is also a place where characters and social coherence have to be developed.

It is, in my opinion, of great importance that those smaller institutions of learning, so beneficial to the development of harmonious personalities, are favored in every possible way. We have to prevent that mass-production is extended to human beings themselves.

(signed) A. Einstein

____

Albert Einstein

69

Brooklyn to Black Mountain
27 January 1955 (postmark)

Charles dear—

It is not what you think—I am so busy I did not even remember you had failed to answer all of my letters—I am very disturbed about you—I am at the moment very unhappy about your magazine, your writing, your relation to life, in fact everything. I disapprove, lock stock and barrel.

So I guess the best thing to do is to meet as I do not even know precisely why I feel so strongly that if you go on in your present ways you are done for—I do not know what it all means to you, but the odor coming off the 3rd volume is a bad odor[5]—everything in it is true, that is saying anything, but a *man*, Charles, should be busy creating something—and it doesn't have to call itself a poem.

I have also been thinking lately a great deal about theatre, its relation to religion, etc. My conclusion varies widely from yours—do not be a Jesuit to your own soul, Charles—

Frances

[on envelope]

Lucinda is dying to see the Tarot Pack.
Please bring.

5 *Black Mountain Review* 3 (published in November 1954) contained Olson's article "Notes on Language and Theatre" and a review of a book on Billy the Kid.

70

Black Mountain to Brooklyn
17 February 1955 (postmark)

Frances!

Much as I damn well love you, & damn well hear you like nobody, there are times like this one when you scream, so even I don't hear you (You shld spell it out if you are going to lay about you that way, my dear girl. What are you chewing my ass off for? For what? That theatre piece? I'd be ahead of you there, but take a look at the Billy the Kid thing in same #—best damn thing I, or anybody's yet said abt U.S.A., I bet

oh, darling: you should yell at me!

But then, I do love you. And just damn well wanted you to know I can't buy this one.

How are you, & Lucinda? Tell her I ain't touched the Tarot since my mother died. Or any magic.

Will send you #4 soon.

All yrs, Charles

71

New York to Black Mountain
26 October 1955 (postmark)

[letterhead: *American Weekly*]

Dear Charles:

Please let me know about yourself—I know you can't, but if you could figure any way to come, I would certainly like to talk to you.

As I see it a very real struggle is going on, underneath all the business, to turn the tide towards the masters, rather than towards the aimless mastered. How many there are, I wonder, but since I built a darling spot in Woodward "a dream house" as Lucinda says, very tiny, but beautiful, I absolutely do not care. I have been seeing some very gorgeous architecture from Italy and am playing around with the idea of going there.

Can't you bum a ride to New York and let me see your architecture once again?

Frances

Part Five

22 FEBRUARY 1956–26 JUNE 1957

When we hear from Olson again he has, by whatever means, accomplished a firm, working tone. He has left Connie and Kate with her sister, Jane Atherton, in Massachusetts and brought Betty and Charles Peter back with him to Black Mountain, a settlement of sorts; but Boldereff is still, in effect, being asked to "hold," as so often in the past.

Boldereff has been carrying two jobs, otherwise we might have seen some probing. As it is, in all the letters of this period it is not clear how much she knows. In any case, she is racing ahead with her own James Joyce studies. We do note with some relief that after Olson's visit of 1–3 June 1957, Boldereff could write that she was "at peace with one's own" (no. 78, 4 June 1957). There was another visit at the end of the month, and then a long gap, which can be accounted for by the fact that, after a year of closing down the bankrupt Black Mountain College, Olson was now making the move to Gloucester, installing his new family in 28 Fort Square.

RM

72

Black Mountain to Brooklyn
22 February 1956 (postmark 23 February 1956)

Black Mountain
Washington's Bday
1956

Frances, my blessed love

When I think that it was you who introduced me to Sam Noah Kramer (whom I am in correspondence with now—since his recent return from East Germany, where he found the 1st map, of Nippur—to bring him here this summer in an Institute of the New Ancient Literature, he and Guterboch, from the Oriental Inst, who is the source of my Hittite poems, to go with my Sumerian ones—the 1st of which is as much your poem as a poem well might be) and that almost to the day you & I came on Martin Sprengling's work on the alphabet (he arrives here next Thursday morning to teach 3rd Century Iran through the Albigensian heresy—via Mani)—

& all

the rest of our identities of this order,

it does strike me, I must say. In fact last night lecturing again for the first time in 9 months (Creeley & Hellman have been teaching writing for three quarters, and I have been bound up with the real estate, cattle sales, and 24 hour miseries of trying to keep a little polis alive in the monstrous bland quantitative present), I caught fire and went 7 hours, and so much I sd abt what went out in 1945 and has come on since—the "in" you and I have (again) both used as the in—sounded as much yrs as mine. In fact yrs, my ears told me, because you are a woman, sounds more right than my own mouthings and firings. For "life" (instead, say, of work, which I might allow I can speak of with a firmness to stay, that is, I did feel what I had talked of most, the word, literally, what is a word, stayed better than any "philosophy", say, which followed) not good enuf[1]

—o Frances, you proved to me 6 years ago what a beautiful thing woman is, that's all—that life is in her fierce attention.

And I wanted this day to lay it out before you as a sort of gift back, a recognition god damn it a statement before you that you are all that you know you are, beautiful Beloved

I want to let it rip to you today—in some funny way I wasn't able to let the seams out directly to you F M B you, the woman, the one whose eyes, the breath, the way you speak the one whose table to let a cigarette burn out on & hurt a thing she prized, the other things (the cedars of you)—I'm saying I let the seams out from the start but it came out then, and since, verse, but now that it has come out some life, I care to tell you—you—the very you who dresses cooks works walks toed in—you, Frances:

yes I did in at least one poem which, if you have the copy please any time give it to me. Like that dream from Montevallo I keep pestering you for. These two things at least, but immediately, the poem, *Epigon*. For I must soon publish it, I think.

(Speaking of that, I have news the past week—double news—which will be as exciting to you as to me: that finally I go into the old island of the speech with colors. And the crazy thing is that it is all what I wld regard as the dirtiest devil poem I have ever written, which knocks the English down (you will recall that Eliot cldn't see his way to have Faber do Ishmael because it was too American for the English, sd he!). But now this new "series poem" O'RYAN has just been asked as a book London;[2] and two days ago Tambimuttu, who is publishing a new magazine "Poetry London-New York" has kept four of the O'RYANS against possible use in his first or 2nd issue.

(Also, just to catch you up, MAXIMUS II (poems 11–22) is in print now in Germany and I shld have your copy to present to you about April 15th, I hope. It is in black, and lovely brickish red, for the cover, and the same type face as I inside, and a like Maillol paper. I think it will be more beautiful but in any case you will see yrself in several of those "Letters," I guess!)

1 Olson's comment refers to all of the beginning of the letter, which he crossed out up to this point.

2 On 13 February 1956, Olson wrote to Gael Turnbull of Migrant Press, Worcester, U.K., accepting his plan to publish *O'Ryan 1–11*, a project that did not finally materialize; likewise the *Poetry London–New York* possibility evaporated.

I despair to tell you what my life now is, simply that it will cause you pain—you even taught me that, that word, and that between us there had to be such pain as the day I got yr letter about Quitman.[3] But then, you knew pain before I did because you knew love, which I had to learn (as you sd so that it took, it was so true, and I didn't know, said you "You don't know anything about love" …

it was true. And now I know a little. I ought to have known better, that I loved you from the start, and have ever, and will, ever

Your Charles my Frances

I enclose an evidence a token an amulet—love love love[4]

[on envelope]

Please write me how you & Lucinda are & what your latest thoughts, readings & doings too.[5]

3 Boldereff's letter of 3 September 1950 (*AMC*, no. 324, pp. 539–41).

4 It is not known what Olson enclosed.

5 Lucy did a drawing of George Washington, which is archived in the file for this letter at Storrs.

73

New York to Black Mountain
26 March 1956 (postmark 26 March 1956)

[letterhead: Westcott & Thomson]

March 26, 1956

Charles—

Too busy to write—was carrying two jobs—got fully exhausted—went up to Woodward to get peace and dream—enclosed[6]—got ill up there—just got back and have started new job as above—very wonderful birthday present—Lucy and I both fine—hope to see you one of these days—sorry to be so really rushed—should calm down later.

Frances

6 The Olson letter from Montevallo containing a dream (not apparently extant).

74

Black Mountain to Brooklyn
13 April 1956 (postmark 14 April 1956)

Friday April 13th 1956

Frances:

You drew me to Rimbaud. And now I am drawn closer and closer to him.

A month ago I used yr translation of Credo and the students were very moved to hear him that freshly (actually I am able to use Schwartz Saison,[7] but only if I control the text by the French; and last week I looked at *seasons, chateaux* in the French, and am under the untested impression that Schwartz is off on the poems, no matter how I can now read the prose out loud and get some of the force of the French.

But that, too, I owe to you.

Just now the voici les temps des Assassins turned what I take to be its proper face to me (quite the opposite of what I take it is the usual reading—that this is some exclamation on AR's part, of a radical position). Coming as it does bang on top of the Hangover passage, and smack after the paean to the marvelous work of the body, I suddenly registered assassination as what he would have been a double-axe towards:

what do you think?

I rushed on to think we ought to do a book on him *together*. But then I remember it's an old idea, and you have shrunk from my taking any exception to your words, silly one. Actually what you say is said, it is always only a matter to me of making it said as us hyar writers do think the word can be made to say more (moveat delectet et doceat: doceat is yours—and my!—forte.

Anyhow, *please*—as I 1st urged you so strongly—put every last thought and flash you have down as a note

7 Arthur Rimbaud's *A Season in Hell*, trans. Delmore Schwartz (Norfolk, CT: New Directions, 1939) was in Black Mountain College library, and later in Olson's.

/ and let same sit, even if you won't show 'em / for every sense you have of said same man is crucial, I take it.

What I was getting at above is I suddenly saw AR as certain on assassins as, say, Dostoevsky was: that they were the time, and yet that such men as those two *knew*

(example, mercy versus justice; mercy is the enfolding of any sufficiency—or insufficiency—in the greater context than the limit of the possibility of anyone. And it doesn't, like charity (caritas) require a leader (the love of God for man)—that, as AR sd, any one of us would want to be the sister of one's death (I think you have this pulled out and there in yr *Minoa*[8]

You know, kill, kill. But I am at war, too. I am certain AR got to that war which can be called Pro-War: the Saison restores Beauty and Charity by the progression itself. And the pivot is Bonheur (n'est-ce pas?)[9]

Let me hear. And how you are. The shift of job sounds as though it was rough again. Let me have your thoughts. And most most thanks for the dream and poem:[10] the poem isn't up to the dream, but the dream stares me in the face.

All my love,

Charles

That word "mercy" can be driven back to what ought now, to replace it:

misericordia

where it came from

(or *misericord*!

Let's right it: "to have passion with, by the heart"

("pity" no good as inactive: mercy is active: but it does not have the stroke in it without the heart as the vulnerable

(why I don't believe AR, at end, was celebrating an Assassin)

8 Olson is referring to the passages from Arthur Evans's *The Palace of Minos*, included in Boldereff's typescript "Credo in Unam" (enclosed with letter no. 59, 2 August 1954).

9 Olson is building up to the poem "Variations Done for Gerald Van Der Wiele," written the following month (*Collected Poems*, p. 396).

10 Boldereff has returned Olson's Montevallo dream letter and the "Epigon" poem.

75

New York to Black Mountain
11 September 1956 (postmark)

Dear Charles—

Have just had the most shocking of experiences. Have been working for some years on Joyce. Finally got a lot of copy ready—thought might mean something. Today I went to the library for fun and happened to get out some notes of Joyce on his play Exiles and these notes are shocking me into my innermost core. In fact they are destroying a universe for me. Either he developed later or I have been reading more Motz than Joyce in Finnegans Wake, because I find from these notes that he is really up in his mind—all up in his mind and saying things that sound exactly like Edmund Wilson and as far as I can tell was not even concerning himself or never even occurred to him that a genuine fight could be put up and a new woman emerge and a new relationship which was not dry and mindish but of living life. Oh Olson I can not express what it all is that is disturbing me so violently, but it is the shattering of many years' joy. Also if it all boils down in the end to literary devices and literary problems, then I see I really must get in there and somehow pitch my own battle and come up with a vision in concrete. I know how to feel it, but—! I will have to go home and examine everything, but there are certain phrases in those notes and after all that is direct to himself, no possibility of misinterpretation that are almost impossible to line up with a living battle *for* something. He seems to be dreaming of the "eternal" feminine in a way which makes me ill all over. O Olson, maybe America is utterly cut off and will have to do the forging without guide or rudder.

I am now perplexed as to how I should conduct myself regarding these fantastically full workings I did on Joyce.

Anyway, a blow I do not at all figure how I am to rise up from under, unless I just sit down and hew away all alone. I saw the movie of Moby Dick which I was afraid to go to see and no matter how inadequate the acting, the movie was marvellous and brought me directly in touch with Melville and for the first time I understood, but precisely, what he means by those dark words I have never understood, "I have written a wicked book and feel spotless as the lamb." Now I know exactly what the wickedness consists in. And I am with him.

Frances

If you can possibly get the Viking edition of *Exiles* with intro by Padraic Colum and notes at end from Joyce *please* get and read because the notes will make it all so clear—it is a *way* of regarding other men—Rabelais, etc.—you know I adore them all and it is somehow as though it was all a *design* problem.

He says—oh well—"Curl the hair anyway you care to and uncurl it again," speaking of women—Oh Olson—never could tell you how embarrassed I am.

76

New York to Black Mountain
5 November 1956 (postmark)

[letterhead: Westcott & Thomson]

Charles dear,

I was sitting working very hard when my landlady knocked and asked if I were home and put your beautiful package on my stair-landing. I was very pleased that it arrived and that it was looking so handsome,[11] also that you had included the list of subscribers because recently I derived such a deep pleasure from reading the list of the subscribers to the Skeat's edition of Chaucer which I recently bought in its entirety and am so delighted with. A most modern man, old Chaucer with ideas about women far more liberal than anyone since as well as about hundreds of other things and what a poet. I am making him my next big passion. The list includes many Americans and this pleases me, too, very much.

Have not had a chance to read all of your book—but do not feel the same force and weight as in the others, the whole thing lighter. If one does not publish for ten years, what does it matter? Was reading a note of DH Lawrence's about all the poems Miss Monroe published that had no reason for being published. That she should have omitted them and my feeling is that I am going to find some of these of that same sort. Rough language, but only means that if you want to be alive, you have to be quiet until the right time comes. For instance the Maximus to himself is very well written, but should have remained to himself, where it really does belong and not be said to anyone, even me. I am sure it is difficult for you down in the lethargy of the non-moving world to feel alive unless you see some action, in the form of publishing, but I feel strongly that if you would leave that place, even to face severe suffering and weld something under all that difficulty you would be better off. I feel that the place is very

11 Olson has sent *Maximus Poems 11–22*, just received from printing in Germany.

bad for you, no matter how perfectly it solves the problem of your family. You can not do your job alone and down there you are alone in a very dangerous way, you receive no criticism and no stimulation and the outward atmosphere is beautiful and there without effort. Not good for you, Olson and you are not right to treat yourself so.

Lucy is away at school this year and I am having fun for the first time in many a long day—expect to get several things off my chest in the years to come, including some Joyce on Shakespeare. But not right away. Now I am going to try to live without a sense of responsibility for a little while, just enjoy.

Your loving Frances

77

Washington to Brooklyn (telegram)
31 May 1957

FRANCES BOLDEREFF
180 CLINTON ST   BROOKLYN NY

HOLIDAY TRAFFIC TOO MUCH COMING TRAIN. ARRIVE CONGRESSIONAL ABOUT SEVEN THIRTY

CHARLES

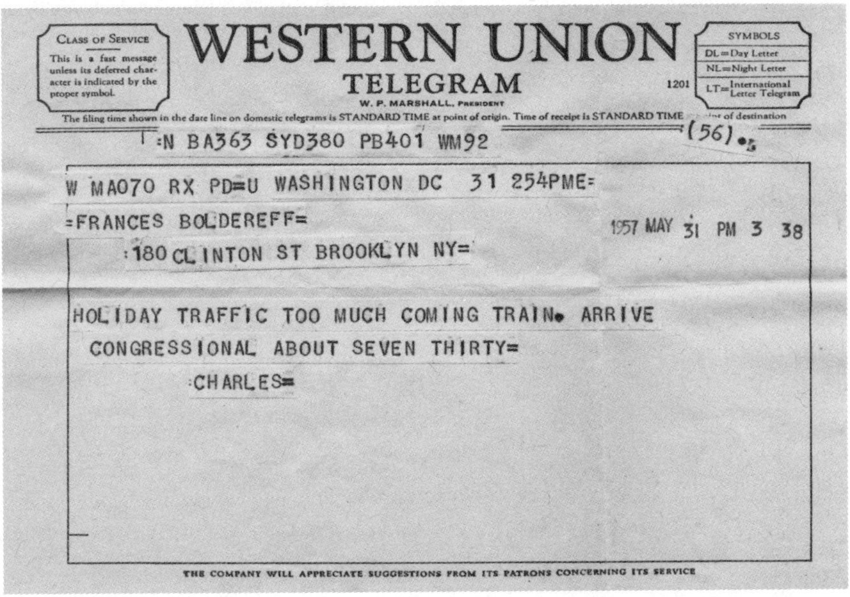

CLASS OF SERVICE
This is a fast message unless its deferred character is indicated by the proper symbol.

WESTERN UNION
TELEGRAM
W. P. MARSHALL, PRESIDENT

SYMBOLS
DL=Day Letter
NL=Night Letter
LT=International Letter Telegram

1201

The filing time shown in the date line on domestic telegrams is STANDARD TIME at point of origin. Time of receipt is STANDARD TIME at point of destination

N BA363 SYD380 PB401 WM92 (56)

W MA070 RX PD=U WASHINGTON DC 31 254PME=
=FRANCES BOLDEREFF=
:180 CLINTON ST BROOKLYN NY=
1957 MAY 31 PM 3 38

HOLIDAY TRAFFIC TOO MUCH COMING TRAIN. ARRIVE
CONGRESSIONAL ABOUT SEVEN THIRTY=
:CHARLES=

THE COMPANY WILL APPRECIATE SUGGESTIONS FROM ITS PATRONS CONCERNING ITS SERVICE

courtesy Lucy Wilner

78

New York to Black Mountain
4 June 1957 (postmark)

Tuesday

Charles—

Nicest kind of sensation, being at peace with one's own. On the surface, utterly sleepy, just hitting me, can not see on the street, moving sort of like a whale, a kind of balloon approach if you visualize what I mean.

This brief note is begging. Remember, daddy, you said I could have a Mardi? Are you going to let me? That is what I was trying to remember when I said there was something else.

My boss is here and I am busy. This is a silent salute.

Frances

79

Black Mountain to Brooklyn
9 June 1957 (postmark 10 June 1957)

Sunday June 9

Frances, my love:

Penogam's awake / Mardi / Muirhead's *Ire*-land off to you,[12] in two packs BOOK POST

Gutted BMC Lib, but only one book looks like any thing: "Celtic Ornament in the Brit. Isles Down to AD 700" by E. T. Leeds, Oxford, 1933, with yum-yum plates. I'll keep to read & bring to you at Woodward![13]

For me too it is now the opening of the flower of my insides because I was with *my own* "*one's own*"—you (and I mean it in the sense I understand you too by "peace" = the joy of love of who is the one

mine,

Charles

Menes (Minos) died of a wasp-bite in the "Land of the End of the Sunset" ("Urani" = "Erin"), claims Waddell ("Egyptian Civilization, Its Sumerian Origin & Real Chronology," L.A. Waddell, Luzac & Co., London, 1930, Chapter IV, pp. 60–70)

Confirmation seen in prehistoric rude grave at Knock-Many or "The Hill of *Many*," near Clogher on the southern border of County Tyrone (ibid, p. 68–9)

Date of death: c. 2641 BC !

PS. Write me, my darling

12 Joyce's *Finnegans Wake*, L. Russell Muirhead's *Ireland* (London: Ernest Benn, 1962), and Herman Melville's *Mardi* sent to Boldereff were perhaps ex-Black Mountain College library copies. Boldereff's copy of *Finnegans Wake* (New York: Viking, 1947) is inscribed "for my Frances and her Joyce love Olson Black Mt June 57" (Frances Boldereff Papers, Archives and Special Collections, University of Connecticut, Storrs).

13 E.T. Leeds's *Celtic Ornament* (London: Clarendon, 1933) remained in Olson's library.

80

Black Mountain to Brooklyn (postcard)
12 June 1957 (postmark)

Don't let this fuss you (knowing such people & such presses)—it suddenly turned up in the mail like a hangnail! Just for yr information!

Love, yrs,
Charles

[The above note was written on a card containing the following announcement]

A CENSUS OF FINNEGANS WAKE
by Adaline Glasheen

The first important guide to the novel in twelve years, with a valuable introduction, a synopsis of the action, a table of "Who Is Who When Everybody Is Somebody Else," and a biographical index to the 5000 characters, historical persons, and mythical figures mentioned in *Finnegans Wake*.

Northwestern University Press, 1956 Cloth $5.00

81

New York to Black Mountain
17 June 1957 (postmark)

Charles dear—

We went to the beach yesterday—and while I kept covered up, my face was exposed and my arms—and today I am like a drunken bum on Brooklyn bridge—red, stiff and swollen and unable to navigate well—anyone who lives away from the fresh air as I do is pretty unlikely to sunburn well—I feel embarrassed, but can do nothing but wait.

I was very glad you sent me the card about Finnegans. It does not bother me because it *sounds*, to one as experienced as I, as though she has put together *things*—does not yet grasp as a whole—it will perhaps make mine difficult to publish or impossible and yet I somehow doubt the adequacy—there is something about the "valuable," "the synopsis" and the "5000" characters which makes me suspicious that Joyce has not been grasped—I am very glad you sent it and after I finish my own, I will read it, but sometimes I get so very angry at the stupid professional twaddle that it actually makes me ill and takes me a long time to recover—so perhaps I will stay away until you look at it and tell me if it is good.

Since Lucinda came home I am unable to do any work—two reasons—I am now alone in my office, so I am not able to get out at lunch time and certainly not for long enough to go to library—then at night, I have to rush home, cook etc and she likes to talk to me—so I have done almost nothing since you were here. However, I did find a poem with the line "Come rest in this bosom"[14]—so it shows that everything in detail is stolentelling and everything in toto is Joyce's. (The poem, by the way, making Joyce's use of the line something utterly exquisite—a poet to his country.)

14 Poem by Thomas Moore.

I am very anxious to see you—if it is not too boring for you to fool around by yourself I should like to have you in Woodward all the time, but it is my last and only opportunity to work—so I must take a good hunk out of every day. I have a clear idea now of how I want to handle this first section, following your suggestion.

Charles dearest. I have carried your note around just to have the contact there—Lucy says she thinks we will always be together. She is very very much on my mind—since the schedule is so unhealthy and food-wise so very inadequate and I feel so cramped and sometimes worried about her strength in adult life—I do wish we didn't live in a world so impossible to balance.

The books have not arrived but I await them eagerly. I think it disgusting that this book had to appear now, but in my interior—am indifferent entirely. It is just that my tight tight financial problems made me *so* want to make a little money.

Will see you very soon—

Your Frances

82.

New York to Black Mountain
21 June 1957 (postmark 21 June 1957)

June 21, 1957

Charles, dear,

You will never know how excited I am about the books which were there last night. The FW arrived a few days ago, but I am too busy to care at this moment. The color is lovely and I am saving it. But this Muirhead's Ireland! O Charles, when I think of the months and months of labor and all could have been solved so easily if I had but had this. However, I have noted one thing—all the books which give such neat and clear descriptions of places are dead—I dug my little bits of odd knowledge out of the nuttiest places and they are all far from the whole or neat story, but each of them breathes with the life of Ireland and gives some flavoring, some smell which conveys a little of what the old master must have felt himself towards that wild and woolly place. I am so thrilled to have this guide that you will just never know, with the thousands of helps, hints, etc. And yet the curious thing is, as I stayed up last night until 2:00 using it, how very few actual entries I can glean from it—Joyce simply does not lend himself, as I have been maintaining for some time, to the encyclopedia hounds, and I am more and more convinced that I do not have to worry about the rivalry of others, since only the reading and reading and knowledge of his soul yields up the real clues.

I am not meaning to convey that because I get few actual entries that I am not thrilled—I just can not tell you how pleased I am—I love it so much I brought it to work with me, although I can do nothing with it, but see its outside. Also, I am thrilled beyond measure to have such a dear little *Mardi*. I am so very grateful to you, Charles. Loveliest package I ever opened, as I adore both my possessions. Lucy thinks I am a howl. Yesterday was my day, for I also got from Ireland the six volumes of

D'Alton,[15] which I carried home last night, and which I did not even look at because I was so excited over yours. Lucy looked and just shook her head in the most adorable way "Nutty mother! what can you do?!"

I have a serious problem on my hands as what to do with my lovely Lucy for the summer, but I think I am going to try to put her in an art class at the Brooklyn Museum, where I believe they have a dining room, where she can eat her lunch. She despises to go anywhere alone and simply will not go to restaurants. It has nothing to do with fear of being alone—it has something to do with the intense admiration she arouses in the male breast and the equally intense modesty of soul she has. She got lost in the subway, on her way home from looking for a job and a policeman came up to help—she reported the conversation word for word, and he must have adored it—she was so indignant and belligerent and modest and I am sure he could hardly believe his ears and must have loved her dear proud independent and so not liking his admiration answers. What a love.
I worry terribly about her health—God will surely have to have her specially in mind if she is to grow up strong and well—so many things are wrong about what I am able to do for her. Among others—o well, just the same, no use to talk.

Uncle Robert's wife has invited you to drive up with me to see that wonderful work he is doing, so I am hoping you will be willing to drive me up to Massena by a beautiful back road from Woodward—I do not think it could be too far and it must be very uncrowded and lovely, from central Pennsylvania straight north thru New York state. I do hope you will take me.

Your loving
Frances

15 Edward A. D'Alton, *History of Ireland from the Earliest Times* (London: Gresham, 1913).

83

Black Mountain to Brooklyn
22 June 1957 (postmark 22 June 1957)

Sat morning
June 22/57

frances:

a lovely phrase for you (to put beside yr daughter calling you a goddess:

You are "wisdom's daughter"!

Love,

the Mixie-
(Maxie)

84

Black Mountain to Brooklyn
26 June 1957 (postmark 26 June 1957)

Wed morning June 26

Frances:

Much as I wld like to have the car in Woodward, things here are dragging so I shall have to come back *after* your vacation, thus I cannot drive up for good. Therefore (if you will realize *driving* has become a damn tedious thing, over distance, in these States) I think now it will be better if I come to Woodward by train.

I regret this, 'cause I think you were looking forward to the car, and it wld have given us a lot of freedom, as well as the trip to Unc Robts'. But please, believe me: even cost-wise, these monster autos ain't worth it (except when you got 'em in yr own barn, like the horse)

Wot's holding me up is the library & the pot shop. Until they were out of the way, & thus the moneys available to the Corporation against its debts, I couldn't settle my personal-legal situation. So it looks now as though I shall have to come back, & maybe be kept here (though not constantly) until the big real estate & money settlements of Sept 21st! (It seems endless)

But I am at the same time leaving my face to regain its innocence, and will come to you more me, I do believe.

Love, my musk,
Charles

Part Six

6 MARCH 1958–8 MARCH 1962

The secret history of Olson's spousal comings and goings is fully revealed in a letter difficult to date (no. 87), but since it was never sent it leaves open the question of when it all came out. Olson was prepared to have Boldereff meet Betty at his Morris Gray poetry reading, Harvard, on 14 February 1962, but the invitation was a last-minute telegram and Olson might have expected that Boldereff would not be able to come. What happened when Olson and Boldereff met on 7 March 1962 in Brooklyn (no. 92) is not known, as there is again a long period of no letters.

RM

85

New York to Black Mountain[1]
6 March 1958 (postmark 6 March 1958)

March 6

Charles—

Rec'd the paperback from Grove Press[2]—I am very pleased they did this—wonderful book and a publisher who has done some nice books—Where are you?

Frances

1 The letter was readdressed to 28 Fort Square, Gloucester.

2 *Call Me Ishmael* (New York: Grove, 1958).

86

New York to Black Mountain[3]
[9 March 1958]

Sunday

I have just finished reading *Ishmael* and find it magnificent. My impressions are so vivid I can not recall what it was you said you had from the new perusal.

I am amazed that I who in a twenty-year-later rereading of Dostoyevsky can find so little I did not find earlier, find such really new things in *Ishmael*. As though I knew neither you nor Melville nor my own thoughts. It is even adding sidelights to my own search—and that not at all in relation to Melville's sex, but in deeper sentences, to be received more osmotically (if that is the word!)

Also I was amazed to realize for the first time—it (Moby-Dick) is the work of a young man—how much that thrills me and explains the marvelous rigor of his passage on the beauty of the movement of a whale's flukes (the chapter called "The Tail" maybe—plus one I do not know where it is). That passage could stand as a text for my life—and on it I could base my entire credo of how man should behave and it seems to me to fit in perfectly with the quote on page 101, "Of old Greek times ..."

There is writing that is perfect and although the prose form is strictly adhered to, in accuracy and daring it is poetic language.

I am very thrilled, Charles, as I was first time and I see you now, as I did then, as a voice the purity of which is not to be disputed.

I can only say I am itching to sit down to my own job—for your book fires me.

Frances

3 The date and place of this letter are conjectural, since there is no envelope.

87

Gloucester (not sent)
[c. 26 June 1958][4]

Frances:

I have loved you the whole time—and have hung myself (not to speak of Con, and now, Bet) believing, the whole time, I would one day live with you, at least give over, to the love, and let it have life to live itself in, instead of staying bottled up in me, and thus doing the harm such wrong does do (Lucinda, a year ago, mistook something I sd, when I took her to breakfast as saying I was a stinker and she sd yes you are. And I sd what! And she sd, a stinker.

At the same time the *facts* are I have lived with Con, and had a daughter. And now have lived with Bet four years, and have a son. (I could excuse not telling you this a year ago by saying Bet left me the day after Memorial Day I came to you;[5] and that we were apart when I came to see you in Woodward. And after. But it is just that I can't tell these things easily, and leave them in time because I am not naturally (am cowardly?) about being direct. Or just straight, with facts.

Ok. To bring it up to date. And to do that to get it open, to open up life between us—as well as for Bet, and myself. (I am not clear that I know anything different than merely to do this—to lay it on the table—that I know any more now than to do this at least. For whatever it means.

In any case, please receive it as merely that: to speak across to you. I miss you, that's for sure. And want to be in touch, in the face of anything. To break any log-jam. That's all. That's what this is. Please write.

My love,
Charles

4 This is a typed sheet inserted into Storrs Notebook 75 "Mostly Spring '58? & summer with end early '59??"

5 31 May 1957. The visit to Woodward was on 26 June 1957.

88

New York to c/o Grove Press, New York
27 February 1959 (postmark)

[letterhead: Westcott & Thomson]

Charles—

I saw Lucy this past weekend and she has begged me to ask you for the return of the picture of Sergie and me—I am sure you can understand why she would want it so very much—a kind of proof to put up in her room, etc—I *hope* it is somewhere where you can find it soon—because Lucy is going through a most unhappy time at present and it would please me to be able to do just this little thing she requested.

I had a copy of your book from Grove Press—which pleased me—saw the poem they issued recently[6] and am full of wonder as to why you took so abrupt a departure and never sent me Maximus—Please be sweet enough to let me hear from you soon.

Frances

6 Grove Press published Olson's poem "The Company of Men" in their *Evergreen Review* 8 (Spring 1959). *The Maximus Poems* (New York: Jargon / Corinth, 1960) was not yet out.

89

Cambridge to Brooklyn (telegram)
27 March 1959

FRANCES BOLDEREFF
180 CLINTON ST BROOKLYN NY

FORGIVE THIS DELAY WILL GET PHOTOGRAPH TO YOU AS SOON AS I CAN LOVE AND FAITH

CHARLES

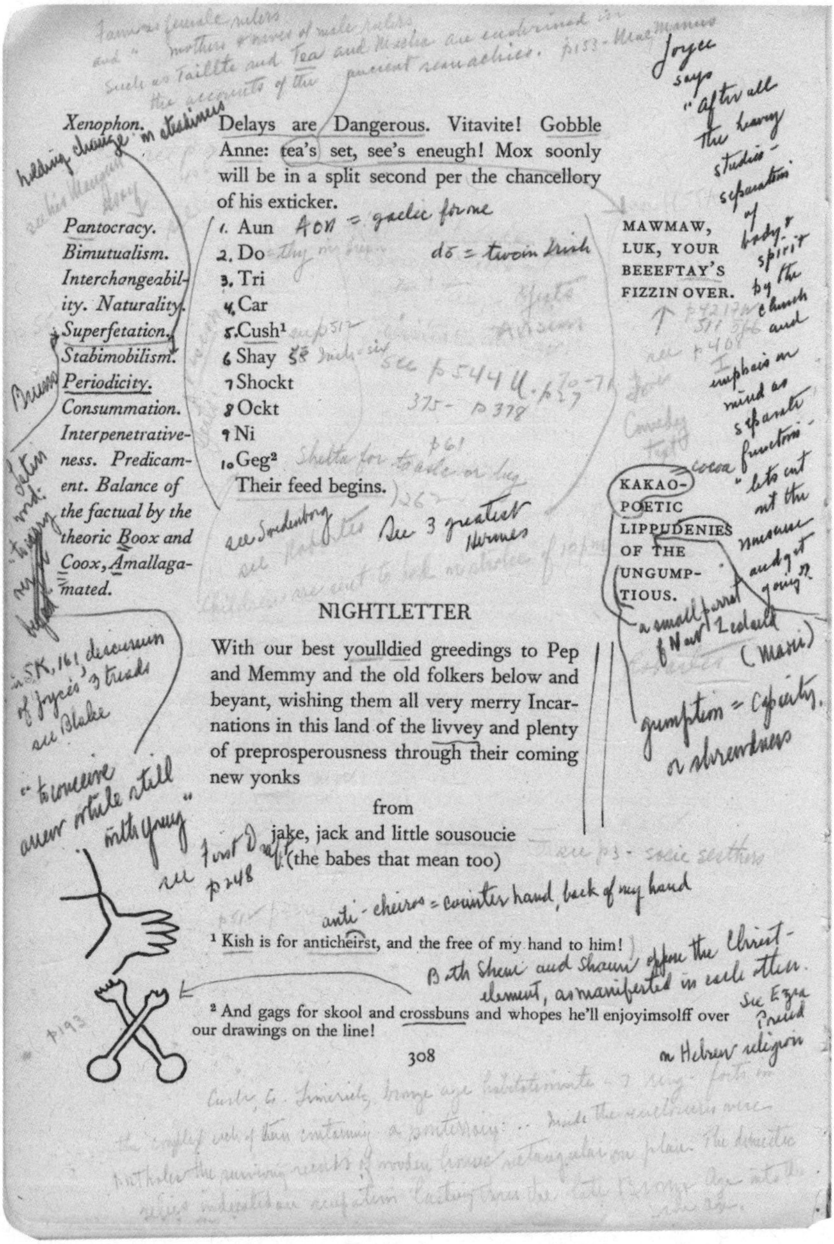

Xenophon.

Delays are Dangerous. Vitavite! Gobble Anne: tea's set, see's eneugh! Mox soonly will be in a split second per the chancellory of his exticker.

Pantocracy. Bimutualism. Interchangeability. Naturality. Superfetation. Stabimobilism. Periodicity. Consummation. Interpenetrativeness. Predicament. Balance of the factual by the theoric Boox and Coox, Amallagamated.

1. Aun
2. Do
3. Tri
4. Car
5. Cush[1]
6. Shay
7. Shockt
8. Ockt
9. Ni
10. Geg[2]

Their feed begins.

MAWMAW, LUK, YOUR BEEEFTAY'S FIZZIN OVER.

KAKAO-POETIC LIPPUDENIES OF THE UNGUMPTIOUS.

NIGHTLETTER

With our best youlldied greedings to Pep and Memmy and the old folkers below and beyant, wishing them all very merry Incarnations in this land of the livvey and plenty of preprosperousness through their coming new yonks

from

jake, jack and little sousoucie
(the babes that mean too)

[1] Kish is for anticheirst, and the free of my hand to him!

[2] And gags for skool and crossbuns and whopes he'll enjoyimsolff over our drawings on the line!

308

A page from Frances Boldereff's annotated copy of *Finnegans Wake*
courtesy Lucy Wilner

90

New York to Gloucester
18 July 1959

Saturday, July 18th

Charles dear,

I was up in Woodward and reading over some old letters and found one which I brought back because I thought you might possibly like it—it seems to me to fit in perfectly with where we are now—where Nietzsche and the archaeologists and Joyce have brought us—and I thought perhaps you might want to use it. To me the passage of Joyce "For when this feeble-bodied figure departs dusk begins to veil the train of the gods, and he who listens may hear their footsteps leaving the world. But the ancient gods, who are visions of the divine names, die and come to life many times, and, though there is dusk about their feet and darkness in their indifferent eyes …"[7] is so intensely moving that I have no words to describe the vivid glimpse I see of Pan, moving off in an atmosphere I know so well, full of mystery and air which seems not for breathing, but for the imparting of secrets and the tight clasp at my innards as I know that I am to be left here alone and can only know he will return. I am not able to describe with words but the actual moment of departure I can feel as though alone in the world.

I am full of things I want to tell—can not you come down some day? I went to the Metropolitan to see those seals from Minoa and they completely usurp me—I can think of no other beauty—for me they have everything—my lovely lady comes from the second city of Troy—

I am in a strange position as regards my book[8]—you see no one can

7 James Joyce, "James Clarence Mangan," *St. Stephen's* i/6 (May 1902), pp. 116–18.

8 *Reading Finnegans Wake*, published by the author in Woodward, Pennsylvania, under the imprint of the Classic Non-Fiction Library, 1959. Olson's copy, now at Storrs, is inscribed "For Charles—A gift in return for so many."

read FW, although they pretend—and so they are unable to gauge my accomplishment—however it has an air to make the experts not dare to argue until they know mine and they are discovering it takes work. Lots of blood went in, Charles—and you say nothing—but I can assure you that despite all the study it represents precisely the kind of knowledge which the Delphic priestess gave off—a kind of plunging down which almost cost me my life and I feel very strongly that Joyce accepts me—in fact it has been a blindfold walk and I could never tell you how indifferent I am to any visible results—I know what is there and I know the future *has* to employ what I have done—I have already had some marvellous responses and I can assure you I want to have it pass quietly from one to another—not be shouted in the marketplace.

Please let me know what you are writing and please send me the second part of *Maximus* which you promised long ago.[9]

Frances

9 Still awaiting *The Maximus Poems* (1960).

91

Gloucester to Brooklyn (telegram)
14 February 1962

FRANCES BOLDEREFF
180 CLINTON ST
BROOKLYN NY

READING HARVARD BOYLSTON HALL AUDITORIUM 430 TODAY WEDNESDAY. WOULD BE VERY HAPPY IF YOU COULD IN ANY WAY MAKE IT.[10] LOVE

CHARLES

10 Boldereff could not attend at such short notice.

92

Brooklyn to Gloucester[11]
8 March 1962 (postmark)

Thursday AM

Charles;

Can not find your address and am just making this up hoping you are well enough known—

I want to have some shirts made for you—and although it is against my principles to let you know, nevertheless it is nonsense for them not to be right—please send me at once your neck size and sleeve length and any other measurement desirable—

You did not write a word in my Maximus book and I was sharply wrenched by your sudden departure[12]—slept solidly and hope you are more at ease than that desperate glance you cast on me as I went to bed would imply.

Ave Maximus, the progenitor.

Frances

11 The return address reads: "Boldereff, 203 Baltic Street, Brooklyn 1, N.Y." The letter is addressed to "Mr. Charles Olson, 26 Old Fort Square, Gloucester, Mass. Postmaster: please forward if address is incorrect."

12 *The Maximus Poems* (New York: Jargon / Corinth, 1960) has no inscription. At some point, Olson sent Boldereff *Maximus from Dogtown—I* (San Francisco: Auerhahn, 1961). He inscribed the volume "for Frances with love Charles." Both volumes are part of the Frances Boldereff Papers, Archives and Special Collections, University of Connecticut, Storrs.

Part Seven

14 JUNE 1964–13 FEBRUARY 1965

The first two letters of this section are Olson's fulsome reply to Boldereff's letter of condolence at Betty Olson's death in an automobile accident on 28 March 1964. The letter had apparently been misplaced for a time (and is unfortunately missing).

Olson is now teaching at the State University of New York at Buffalo with enough salary to allow him to go where he pleases and with whom. There are a couple of trysts with Boldereff, but it seems that they decided it was as it had always been: that to live apart was the more productive thing. Yet Olson in his loneliness is increasingly ardent, saying in one letter (no. 95, 12 July 1964), "I want to come to see you soon, and with the same desire & reason." Then, in her reply, Boldereff drops a rather large bomb: she has suddenly pledged herself to somebody else, "someone more truly Maximus than yourself" (no. 97, 9 September 1964). Now we get a chance to hear Olson roar!

RM

93

Wyoming, NY, to Trenton
14 June 1964 (postmark 15 June 1964)

My dear beloved woman you are *hopeless*! Here suddenly *Sunday night June 14th* I get around to look over the dirty mail—institutional mail, and I think Van Nostrand a textbook house & out in front of me comes the words of the woman whom I would turn to always in my life—and she sounds like some goddamn hostess, preaching & making side remarks! If I didn't love you like the Earth itself it wld *bother* me that you write letters—all but one, & a few more!—like an idiot: you are sticky Frances Motz with your little nose in the air. Good God what's wild is this weekend suddenly I *wasn't* making it with my little 9 year old son & a very gifted—one of the few blue-eyed persons I ever knew who's eye I can yield some trust to—saw that the kid was blue again (she's done it once before) and took him off leaving me with the measurement of the exact 150 miles to Woodward—
& all the time there in the mail was *where you are*—at least!
You are too much, and of course always was am etc. & this is simply—as always—to tell you to drop it and give me the utter joy of hearing from you as soon as possible seeing you loving you as I never have ceased

Your own

Wyoming, New York, is where I am, & reaches me direct—and the telephone, in case you are wealthy (I *am*, though god knows it's the 1st time, & I don't know how long I can *make* it) is *HYacinth 5-2251* and don't be bothered if you get a busy signal. I leave it off the hook all the time I'm in bed—or am at least retired.

How is Lucy? I often think of her, especially in her belief you & I belong in hyphen anyway forever—as in fact for me it is so—how is she? and what's up in her life too? Give her my fondest (as well as thank Elizabeth, for that how come she shld see a newspaper? is she & her husband in this *neighborhood*???

Anyway, Frances: shut-eye and all the love the world bears,

Charles

PS

You've the biggest high-falutin bag—& I'm not drunk except with finding a letter from you whom I believe is just what I say you are the most beautiful thing ever was or ever will be—what a creature etc whom I love desperately & hopelessly etc etc *only* you talk shit & I cld ram it down your blessed throat

(this sounds as sexy & defamatory as that letter Duke stole or destroyed, & my balls start the same way saying it. So there we are, dear wonderful thing! There's no use I do think so & even if I *always* think you are *wrong*—like you was are wrong on Michelangelo it doesn't at all altogether matter somewhere gloriously *else*.

So—scrawling like you used when you waz going like crazy.

Yr permanently new lover

Charles

AND what are *you* doing besides designing professors of mathematicses books? Like who needs mathematics *today*—I mean literally having *today* this very day examined lexis or better actually *Epitedeumata*

What is the latest thing your own wonderful I mean your *soul* not your nose has got you into—besides daily brilliance of OCCUPATION—the most recent book, on Oscar Wilde?

Your sour old dog face
hombre from outer space,
Charles the Man
Olson

94

Wyoming, NY, to Trenton
15 June 1964 (postmark 15 June 1964)

Wyoming, Monday
June 15th
1964

My dear Frances,

Simply realize of course that all I wanted to do was tell you anything—& I do think that way about you

I very deeply love your letter to me on Bet's death and wish to God I had received it when it was written[1]

Please write,

Your
Own

Charles

1 The letter is missing.

95

Gloucester to Princeton
12 July 1964

July 12th

Frances, That night in Lewistown[2] *alone* should have shown you that any such impression as you had of my last visit to you in New York was wrong on *both counts*[3]—or any such dopey finicalness about how you are yourself (which you've been putting in my way for years): I love to sleep with you forever you great finical idiot (who won't stop to pee in a great open field outside your own house in Woodward—and had me completely trying to hold my shit while we lived together there ourselves. Let's for Christ sake get this straight: that I always come to sleep with you with the greatest will a man can have, and to settle that once & for all: I want to come to see you soon, and with the same desire & reason

Your own ultimate & forgiven lover, Charles

2 Presumably Lewistown, Pennsylvania, near Woodward.

3 In an interview with Tom Clark, Boldereff recalls a rendezvous with Olson in New York City, where he talked all through the night: "He was in terrible psychic suffering, but I couldn't respond. There was no contact between us. I felt, there's no human being there, just a husk. He was experiencing a real loss of his own identity, which he was hoping to get back through me. Alas, it did not work" (Tom Clark, *Allegory of a Poet's Life* [New York: Norton, 1991], pp. 313–14).

96

Gloucester to Trenton
31 August 1964 (postmark 1 September 1964)

August 31st 1964

Frances,

Simply to ask you to ignore anything about that previous letter which cut you off from me.

Charles

28 Fort Square
Gloucester, Massachusetts

97

Woodward to Gloucester
9 September 1964 (postmark 9 September 1964)

[letterhead: Book Design / Frances Boldereff / Woodward, Penna.]

Wednesday September 9

Charles dear—

Here I am, same place, same thing—trying to woo carpenters into doing a little work for me and washing the faces of my dear baby fruit trees, tender and tempting to all living things, who gnaw and suck and chew them avidly!

Charles—awful—but I must tell you I have already pledged myself to someone—someone more truly Maximus than yourself—whose ancestors came from whaling men at Sag Harbor and who lived alone as a very young boy with Indians—ran off and was literally adopted into an Indian tribe and went very far north, almost to top of Canada with them, living alone and apart but always traveling with them by canoe and by foot and initiated by them into the arts of silence, faultless hearing, seeing, etc. A man three years older than myself who is younger than anyone I know—and we are buying a house together—

It seems unbelievable to be writing you this from Woodward but this recent event is perfect for me—has absolutely nothing to do with love—has to do with speaking an identical language about daily modus vivendi—

This crazy place may someday be comfortable but at the moment I am struggling under thousands of "must-do's"—needless to say—once settled, shall be delighted to welcome you.

It seems ridiculous that life so turns itself around—couldn't be more surprised were the skies to fall—but it is really so.

Frances

98

Gloucester to Brooklyn
12 September 1964

Frances:

That's the worst news possible—and I don't have any idea what it is going to be like to live without the thought of you as mine. But one thing I'm sure of: I am Maximus, and your husband, whoever he is and however fine I am God help me sure he must be, simply because he says he is, and proves it to you, is not. He is somebody else and don't please ever continue to mix such things. I am absolutely angry there, that you have no business ever ever ever using—any more than God help me I pray I ever have—you, mixed over with somebody else. Or appropriated, to your own purposes. These are wrong things, Frances—and you have a tendency (things mixed), to put it the least, to do that. (You did the same thing the very first afternoon we were together—& here you are *still* doing it. Wow. I for God sake believe we did belong together completely & utterly & I can prove what you yourself wrote on my copy of your book *myself. BUT: don't DO. THAT Dig*? Do you dig? uh?) (This is the MUSH OF "*NATURE*", INDISCRIMINATELY *PERMITTED*—You SLOP REFERENCES God damn you—*also*.) Please don't—or, and again I do as forever believe also that what you do is beyond compare—this man can be exactly what you now tell me he is. That's fine. And God help my soul I love you so much I am glad God help me you have just what you want but please don't mix things please don't. I don't think you do. Or at least I never for a minute didn't think you were the cleanest thing I could imagine but you are a bitch (*and very wrong*) when it comes to the things other people do which you utterly utterly utterly don't prove your right to & thus you say these sloppy stupid things you say which *are* (*abuse*) the other person's. That no one can do, and get away with it. Not on *your life* even yours, Frances—and I love your life and respect it to the tips of my nature.

Ok God damn it. Blessings altogether. I wish I were he, & I dreamed of a life just like what you two now imagine for yourselves and I can't stand it that I've lost it to this latest thing of your life but I hope and believe altogether that it is and will be just what you yourself can always be. Love and forever Charles

OK. I wanted to have these things said truly. For I do love you and I am very very happy if you are. Isn't this unbearable.

Well Blessings—I mean *altogether*. Good God. It sounds wonderful. I mean wonderful. Yours for keeps, you dumb remarkable wonderful perfect but also fucking stupid & impossible bitch—on *one score alone*, your very *poor tongue*, *very poor tongue* (lengua *morality*) of *tongue*

Rest of letter:

You can talk—& I can testify to that, as well as to all the other things you are beyond belief beautiful in—but *you are absolutely unwilling yourself*, & *in your life* to take the risk of *the very acts of the men you have spent your life using the words of* and reading & paying attention to. What *do you* make of that? Wow, Frances: this is the #1 fact; and I *hate* you for mixing *my words* up with another man *who*—as you so plainly say—has got a virtue I certainly *in particular*, by your own admission, have no reason not to believe in & respect. But you—because you are hung here, *don't use your tongue*, in fact, have no confidence in your use of language: but you don't *leave* it there. You take *men's* use of language. And *then!*—look what you do here: put this other poor man up—rack him up, on *listening*. Wow. And *compare him* to me!

OK. My God I wish *to God* it was possible to make you read this as though it wasn't, in fact, aroused by this occasion. *Which*, *in fact*, it *isn't* at all—I know you, Frances, and I know myself. And I believe in both of us (as you have *more often* been the stater of the fact). What is wholly *offensive*—even in this happiest of possible events—except for me, like—is that *again*, *as forever* you have to use *my creation my* work—wow—as the *measure* of your true new man. That, my dear, doesn't go. Don't you *know* that? I've tried to tell you, time & time again, from your *first* book on (& many of our own events pivot on your doing the same thing—your *flapping* tongue, which, even, I love, and have been present to, time and time again, even knowing *both in print and in event* why you do *it*, what it is which leads you to take other (!) *men's work* & *words* for your own)—no, Frances, it doesn't & it won't go down. Please believe me here. I love you & would stand to the world on you and your behalf, and hope I will take, as well as have any occasion you may—or *anyone else*—present to me to show that. But this *one thing*—& I've never seen you fail to do it (which is why I am begging you to *erase it* as of this new departure into a life with a man whom I am sure I would both love and understand (if for no other reason than that you do! Like indeed I do love Boldereff himself, in his life, & Duke—and Quitman I'm sure, whoever really you have loved. That's not the point. The point is you—and God knows I still *don't know* that you *do* know—*abuse ON THE VERY POINT YOUR WHOLE DEVOTION AND ACT OF LIFE OTHER THAN YOUR LOVE-MAKING* from the very beginning—do try to hear me—have *DEVOTED YOURSELF TO MEN OF LANGUAGE.*

Hear me, Frances.

I am *the live one* of the lot, and you can trust me: don't use their lives work words or beliefs as *though they were yours*, in that literal property or possessive (possession) sense—that they *transfer*, that way, by some act of the decalcomanie of the senses, over to your own beautiful body. They don't. I know damn well and *can prove it*, that your boast, of what your love-making can do *for any man* at all I should think, can do. That's not any more at issue than for example the probable beauty of this man (you have not named, curiously enough) but whom I'm sure is everything you say about him. I don't have *any doubt* loving you. And knowing you. None whatsoever. BUT I WLDN'T, FOR A SPLIT SECOND—& you've just again, in this letter to me today, proved it—*TRUST YOU* WITH ANY *MAN'S WORDS ON YOUR TONGUE*. How about *that*? No really, Frances—How abt that? *how* abt even the way you abused (and you *know* it, & you know *I* know it) that Hanser (Hancher? Hanford?) or somebody's name fellow the President of Iowa,[4] when you were having Lucinda *do you see what I mean*? please? that you *aren't* sure? Therefore—& you *know* this by the *perfectness* of your own acts otherwise (altogether I wld love to prove!)—that ISN'T the way *LIFE* is. And *that*, the truth.

Okay. Please—I suppose I'm

scared now, that, we'll never have again the chance to be as close. Or confidential. And I have loved you with all my life. And I don't know now where in fact to place that life or what in fact to do with it in all those ways at least you were my dream of it. That I can say. But in fear that I may never have again the chance to address—as my heart and soul have always dreamed of doing—your own (to me) utterly boundless, and beautiful (beyond compare) self—you made my own life a revelation to me because you were so beautiful—and I have never believed (& don't now stop!) that my own in touch with yours, always going out—and in the depth just being with you, gave it, so that all I had to do, *really*, in life, was

4 Presumably Olson refers to Virgil Melvin Hancher, thirteenth president of the University of Iowa. The context of this situation is not known.

to open up myself to you—So, my love, because I don't want ever to be cut off from you but also can't see at the moment why from now on it must be different, I beg you to hear me say *only* this one thing I have herein. And *again* only because you *provoke it*. You are *not* free, my beloved Frances, to use the cry of men's lives, and work, as though *theirs* were *yours*. You have your own, my beautiful one—and some of those of yours are like yourself, & like the clothes you make for yourself. And above all your *acts* are yours. That's for sure. But not any of those appropriations from *another man's life & words*: they *aren't yours for use*. For the simplest reason: you haven't paid for them. You've paid for your life, that's sure. That's *not* it. But you can't use or abuse any life—to clear, or support your own. Not at all. And don't kid yourself here. There *isn't* any way you can appropriate words any more than you *well know*—even beyond most persons probably—or *all*, to my loving eyes the *proof*, of *your* life. Wow. I think that it is the most—with that *one* exception. And I don't even think (as I say) you know that—that you do do something which isn't *yours to do*. Wow. Imagine. I think you *more than anyone* do do what is *yours* to do. I love that in your life & love you, and your life, for it. But when
you make
comparison,
or studies
you are doing a thing which is *not equal* to what you do, with your mouth shut or open (except in this one instance, of what I call *the right of tongue*) when you use somebody else's life or words as a reference comparison measure. Here your own
is altogether
good enough. Leave this man,
and mine—and *each man's*, *any man's* whom you yourself find valuable as in fact you most decidedly can claim to have, your life equally
treated

very very

special. I love you, and hope altogether for every thing you do, and for all the future. Your lover (forever

the *only man*,

who knows enough,

to tell you

—off! Your own Charles Olson, from
the first letter from
WOOD-
WARD

Charles

Saturday
September 12th
1964

My address—in case we can continue to be always you and me—is always from here—*28 Fort Square*, but directly I shall be unfortunately in Buffalo (where I have no address at present). So please, if you care to tell me how all does go—or anytime—*always* write me Gloucester, and it will come to me. Hoping you will (and *hoping for all* dreams for you too,

Charles

99

Fort Hunter to Trenton[5]
14 September 1964 (postmark)

Fran:

Here I am in your kind of country—and that is a shocker, your news. I'm happy—for you, and your friend is, as they say, at a launching, a lucky / guy. Only of course he is *not* Maximus. And you are again guilty of your literary associations. *I* am Maximus—and may Hell yawn for you because you don't leave things alone. I love you altogether except for this silly thing which has also dominated your life. But you are beautiful, and I wish anything for you.

Yours,

Charles

5 Olson was on his way to Buffalo by car, writing to Boldereff on the back of a manila envelope that contained a copy of *A Bibliography on America for Ed Dorn* (San Francisco: Four Seasons, 1964), inscribed: "Frances: So long as you have fruit trees here, and I did keep you from going to Russia, here is a reason. Yours, LXIV Charles Gloucester September 12th" (Frances Boldereff Papers, Archives and Special Collections, University of Connecticut, Storrs).

100

Buffalo to Trenton (not sent)[6]
13 October 1964

Beloved Frances

I am asking the Commonwealth of Pennsylvania to send you something. If you will put the two parts together I hope you will think they are as handsome as I do. At least I think they belong peculiarly to you.

Love in all you do,

Charles

October 13th,
1964

6 This letter is torn into eight pieces, which seems to indicate that Olson changed his mind about sending whatever gift he had in mind.

101

Trenton to Buffalo
13 February 1965 (postmark 13 February 1965)

Saturday February 13

Olson my dear—

Courage, mon enfant.

Something tells me I am going to unfasten the bonds—

You might let me have some kind of telephone number—

Frances

Part Eight

20 MARCH 1965–28 MAY 1969

This final section opens with Olson's steady voice, steady in his affection; but when he flies to Italy to appear at the Festival of Two Worlds in Spoleto, he seems to disintegrate at being without a travelling partner (no. 105, 28 June 1965). Of course, he pulls himself together for the European events and the Berkeley Poetry Conference afterwards. Back in Gloucester, he is integrated enough to be very gracious in welcoming Boldereff's hard-won volume, *A Blakean Translation of Joyce's Circe* (no. 108, 21 August 1965), though there have been many hints along the way that the subject is not one he would normally be drawn to.

Then again abroad, this time in Britain and Germany, Olson feels desolate: his heart lies at Boldereff's feet and he wishes she shared his bed. But this is from a safe distance. And this seems to be the pattern till the end. When Boldereff is flushed with producing her amazing book *Hermes to His Son Thoth*, Olson buys five copies for friends, but is not present with the champagne. He is committed to his daily work alone in the top rooms of 28 Fort Square, Gloucester. His last letter, from the solemn distance of the path to the grave, is totally a love letter.

RM

My dear Frances,

I hope to the Lord you don't feel I stood you up. Actually this working for a living leaves me with so much piled up that I had, somewhere, to stop if possible. And catch-up. Or at least try to get some work done. - (I'll know soon what the future will be; and it will also be spring.

Please write to me, even if I judge you are still involved with Tantalus. Or his son. (I don't mean that pejoratively). Both of those men are also my own heroes, and I follow their 'courses' as I do my own year.

What are you up to? (You know, of course, that you are my Goddess too, and I wish you would lay yourself out to me, on anything: I find more from what you are, or do, or read, or think

Love,

or wear, or say -

isn't it marvelous?

Yours,

Charles

Sweet salmon,
from the clearest coldest
waters, cut the finest
on the bone
                Rose
directly
from the stream, straight into my greedy
throat. And breast. A home,
for life, Wise Goddess

of the straightest
sapling

(for You, again, March 20th,
1965)

courtesy Lucy Wilner

102

Buffalo to Trenton
20 March 1965 (postmark 21 March 1965)

My dear Frances,

I hope to the Lord you don't feel I stood you up. Actually this working for a living leaves me with so much piled up that I had, somewhere, to stop if possible. And catch-up. Or at least try to get some work done. —(I'll know soon what the future will be; and it will also be spring.

Please write to me, even if I judge you are still involved with Tantalus. Or his son. (I don't mean that pejoratively. Both of those men are also my own heroes, and I follow their 'courses' as I do my own year.

What are you up to? (You know, of course, that you are my Goddess too, and I wish you would lay yourself out to me, on anything: I find more from what you are, or do, or read, or think

Love,

or wear, or say—

isn't it marvelous?

Yours,

Charles

Sweet salmon,
from the clearest coldest
waters, cut the finest
on the bone
Rose
directly
from the stream, straight into my greedy

throat. And breast. A home,
for life. Wise Goddess

of the straightest
sapling

(for You, again, March 20th,
1965)[1]

1 This poem was included by the editors in *The Maximus Poems* (New York: Jargon / Corinth, 1960), p. 440, and *The Maximus Poems Volume Three* (New York: Grossman, 1975), p. 72.

103

Buffalo to Trenton
24 June 1965 (postmark 25 June 1965)

Beloved Frances,

Life is awful. And if anything in your own life should lead you to send anything to me—actually literally I suppose I mean yourself—I should be relieved to know it. Or receive it.

Simply to tell you how beautiful you are, in my mind, and how thoroughly—and by perfect dream—I do love you,

Your
Charles

departing Buffalo, Thursday
June 24th

104

Rome to Trenton
27 June 1965 (postmark)

[letterhead: Hotel Atlantico]

Dear Mother Woman, Love you more than Ever, Having Flown Through the Empyrean and Arriving here in the Host of Human beings.—Incredible rush of Ancient Human Life, the light soft close beautiful condition of every possible matter, trolley cars, old dirt walls, hay (made into perfect solid houses on edges of fields—(the clouds above the Earth also Mad; and the Sun in Lisbon Awaked Me Into Farther Life

—Am here, to go today to Spoleto, to read there this week, through Friday, and then, according to plan, cross over to Bled, in Yugoslavia, for the International Congress of the PEN—for five days.

Would you *write me*? I would—I crave—to hear from you, and Gloucester won't reach me fast enough. Frances, sit right down write me *air mail* (stamps enclosed—15c per half-ounce)

1st, care of Festival of Two Worlds—*de due Monde*—Spoleto, Italy; &, 2nd, care of International PEN, Bled, Yugoslavia

All my love, & if ever wish you were here had meaning I can assure you today its meaning is ultimate, Love, Your Slave,

Charles

PS (1) Heat here yesterday put me out of my Mind—Was like the Blast from the heat of Jet Engines.

PS (2) Are you all right? and can you give me *news* of yourself? And also keep in *constant* touch?

PS (3) I need to know everything about you to plan my own future directly after 10 days from now!

PS (4) Bombard Me, Please

105

Spoleto to Trenton[2]
[28 June 1965]

love & despair, to tell you how completely as I said to you yesterday, I wish forever & altogether you were with me.

I arrived here yesterday afternoon, by train from Rome—2 hours, in a very wicked heat (there) And was thrust almost immediately into this "*Festival*"

—~— —~—

jaws at dinner last night on (the last time I was in Italy)[3] Viva Duce
Our Duce etc

Fortunately I do not have to do anything today but write to you, look out this window / am now sitting in the sun, writing on my lap. waiting

—~— —~—

in my life, & our joie

impressive (?) presence in the music-box of an equally lovely Teatro C. Melisso of such bald-headed Europeans as Quasimodo, Neruda, Rafael Alberti—& snow-haired Stefan Spender
Spendare

—~— —~—

2 The fragments that constitute this letter are on six sides of torn paper, i.e., the front and back of the lower third of three sheets of paper.

3 Olson did a ten-week tour of Europe as an oratorical contest prize in the summer of 1928.

to that other absent fact only: that you *aren't* here. Oh Frances my Deliverance *my* "*France*"

All right. Another hour. Please love me forever also. Your straw in any of these beautiful valleys of Man, Your "Frances" (if you

Blake correctly says, there is none which man doesn't create: so it is with me you are: I am created in love because you are the smells of the utter night the enormous unimaginable 13th century "leap" of the

106

Princeton to Bled, Yugoslavia[4]
3 July 1965 (postmark)

[letterhead: D. Van Nostrand Company, Inc.]

Charles dear—

Am glad that ancient beauty still shining—would be thrilled to be there—

Out of the blue early this year my very dependable body gave signs of all the hell it has taken—I was sitting on my sofa and a strange pain in my back—anyway paid no attention but it spread and increased and finally I thought I had some awful disease like cancer—pain spread throughout interior—odd!—anyway went to a really nice doctor in New York who cured me quickly—so thinking I was better, I walked from 42nd E to 60th very West and back again to buy some tickets for Russian theatre—well, started all over again and after x-rays discovered I have a disintegrated disc above sacrum, which is big bone like a butterfly sort of across hips—where *everything* feeds into spine—so anyway—now I am in situation where if I walk a little too far—or anything—pain starts up—don't care about pain but I *saw* the x-ray and what is to prevent its finally wearing right through I can not see—anyway—I enjoy my liberty while I can because my guess is freedom of movement won't be possible to me forever—strange that both of us should suddenly *know* we have mortal flesh—it changes a considerable amount of my thinking—I am fixing up Woodward as fast as I can because how long I can go on working I do not know—

I am still planning to be married, but have not absolutely made up my mind—however, you should not count on me in any way—as my guess is I will sit still in my house and work on my new book—married or unmarried—

4 This letter arrived at the PEN International Congress too late and was returned by the post office.

My *Blakean Translation of Joyce's Circe* is out in the stores[5]—has sold remarkably well—with some very lovely anecdotes—I seem to have created some friends out there among Joyce lovers—Lucy's art on cover—I think you will love it—hope so—have no agent in either Gloucester or Buffalo—but it is everywhere in New York—Doubleday at 57th and the other one near there—50? Scribner's, H Br W, Brentano, 8th St Bookshop and a million other ones—paperback—I am handling entire thing myself with agents—no advertising.

Thrilled you were at Spoleto and hope you can somehow not be upset—heavy kind of problems to handle. What can I say? Am embarrassed because I feel that I will go on with Mulford[6]—

Frances

I answered this at *once*.

5 Frances Boldereff, *A Blakean Translation of Joyce's Circe* (Woodward, PA: Classic Non-Fiction Library, 1965).

6 The publisher of *Time as Joyce Tells It* by Reighard Motz (one of Boldereff's pseudonyms) is listed as Mulford Colebrook Publishing of Mifflinburg, Pennsylvania.

107

Trenton to Gloucester[7]
31 July 1965 (postmark 31 July 1965)

2010 Lawrence Road
Trenton NJ
08638

Saturday

Charles dear—

Where are you?
Why didn't you give me any place to reach you?
If you are home call me up.
If not, write.

Frances

7 Boldereff misaddressed the letter to "Stage Fort Avenue," Gloucester, and although it was marked "Addressee unknown," it finally found Olson.

108

Gloucester to Trenton
21 August 1965 (postmark 21 August 1965)

Frances, Your book is absolutely beautiful,[8] and I am—was, last night, on arrival (Friday, August 20th) delighted to read it—and have it. (The preface itself says—in fact as is *always* true, when the person is such as you, the knowledge of yourself as therein stated, without recourse to proof other than the common truth so there is therein statement itself, is so beautiful I hope you will write always straight out from yourself.

I only wanted to speed this note to you in the midst of dishes, & a sick stomach, & seeing my son again, to tell you I hope you can give me other or *more* ration than these coming three days Monday Tuesday Wednesday—even though my heart & soul—and body—rush pell-mell to be there.

Also found your letter of August 1st addressed—miracle of miraculousness that you should have *that* address—"Stage Fort Avenue"—

Anyway, *very* excited to continue to read you as soon as I can get back into my room, your own
Charles

8 Olson's copy of *A Blakean Translation of Joyce's Circe* (at Storrs) is inscribed "For Charles, because he 'holds hard' Frances."

28 Fort Square, Gloucester, Massachusetts

Kate Olson Archive

109

Gloucester to Trenton
22 August 1965 (postmark 23 August 1965)

Frances,

I was so excited to have your generous inscription I didn't mention it. (I'm still so completely attracted to your "argument," in the Preface, of a contraction AND, that until I have that—or anyway I *do* have the difficulty, which you will know, that I don't or haven't again read Joyce enough to do more than scan your own notes for *your self*. And you mustn't mind that. The Blake anyway is happily now my own. And so I am in perfect position to read anything of *his* shot—I mean *his*, and no commentator actually: I'm only actually at that stage. Or, in fact (as Creeley so wisely said in a letter in today) criticism of any sort seems just now—or at least for those of us who are at this point in 1965, not as important as something the word statement (and I think I used it in my note to you Saturday) does supply—

Love & hope you are enjoying
what I imagine are three days off??
Write me please
Your Charles

110

Gloucester to Lawrenceville[9]
29 August 1966 (postmark)

Frances—

Please at least let me know where you *will* be, if you *are* going away for the month of September

—and I have another book to send you which, though it is in English, I *hope* you will find the style of the publication as interesting (though it *isn't*[10]

—nor as good as a 3rd one in today which tho small is one of the *few* pleasures I have ever had from publishing[11]—

When will *you* do a book by me?? I at least dream of that

Love to Lucinda as well—please keep me on to all of yourself.

Your Old Man,
Charles

[on envelope]

Also: in case you may be near a television set they tell me I shall be the subject of a half hour show Poets USA National Educational Television (Channel *13*—?) week of Sept 4th

Charles

9 Addressed to "Frances Boldereff, 19 Hendrickson Road, Lawrenceville, N.J."

10 Olson had previously sent the German edition of his poems *Gedichte,* trans. Karl Reichert (Frankfurt: Suhrkamp Verlag, 1965) with the inscription "Frances: love, Charles." The other book was *Human Universe and Other Essays,* ed. Donald Allen (San Francisco: Auerhahn, 1965).

11 *'West'* (London: Goliard, 1966) had arrived from England. Olson sent Boldereff a copy with his letter of 15 November 1967 (no. 119).

III

Berlin to Lawrenceville
30 December 1966 (postmark 1 January 1967)

[letterhead: Hotel Steinplatz]

December 30th (1966)

Frances love,

Simply to tell you. And that your Maenad (with double flute) came into my hands, with its endearing message, only yesterday—even too late, for my 56th birthday!

I am poised here on the tilt (of the East) only to gather strength (I hope) to go into those places my mind has fed on, as have yours. And which now lie open before me—casements, wasn't it, Keats called magic casements opening on seas forlorn (?)—

In any case my heart lies at your feet—And I wish you shared my bed. And life.

Happily, & Eternally Yours

If you wld ever write you can reach me [Olson draws attention to the letterhead with a line] for at least another fortnight.

112

London to Lawrenceville
30 April 1967 (postmark 1 May 1967)

[letterhead: The May Fair Hotel]

Sunday April 30th

Frances—

Please write me here, to learn if you are all right etc—I *last* was in touch with *anyone* the day your letter came telling me you had been fired. Since, I have been isolated from all contacts, so *even* if you got the book (from Hoyem) I don't know what you thought![12]

Also: anxious to know if you are making it—

Please

Charles

12 On the evidence of an envelope from Andrew Hoyem (publisher, Auerhahn Press, San Francisco) to Frances Boldereff, dated 16 March 1967, *Human Universe* was sent on that date.

113

Lawrenceville to Gloucester
1 November 1967 (postmark)

November 1

Charles dear—

I went down to the door to have the postman hand me my mail and he handed me your book[13]—they have done such a very nice job with it—I am truly pleased—and I will reread it as books are different things at different times.

Today is my first day at home—I have had the honor to be fired once more—my 165th time! At the moment I am working on my new book which is already at the printer's[14]—have proof of two chapters—very tough going for the typesetter—

I am reading Paul Klee with whom I have become enamoured—and I am trying to rewrite Preface to my book—*Where* to get my hands on necessary cash no idea at moment—!

Thought I was going to Woodward this weekend but the darling kids who were driving me can not go.

Thanks very much for sending me the book and let me know what you are working on—

My own thing excites me so terribly sometimes I find it hard to breathe—and I love it how all the death in the air confronts these guys now face-to-face—I saw Reston the commentator on TV the other night with that face with its ugly deep lines—and he was saying about Fidel Castro "I have to admit there *is* enthusiasm" and then pictures of Fidel

13 The Cape edition of *Call Me Ishmael* just in from London was inscribed "Look, what brought you to me Love Charles November 1, 1967."

14 *Hermes to His Son Thoth: Being Joyce's Use of Giodorno Bruno in Finnegans Wake* (Woodward, PA: Classic Non-Fiction Library, 1968).

haranguing away—I wish I could have seen more but it was handled in a way very hard to make out what was going on.

Frances

p.s. I never received any letter. Did you send one?

114

Lawrenceville to Gloucester
1 November 1967 (postmark)

same day—8:30 pm

Charles—

I have reread it all—it is a great book.

And now, along with the reawakened ache in the sense of Melville's suffering I realize two things—that by his suffering Melville helped get us clear, at least of that clinging to the white thing and

2. that I read your book very deeply—because after that first time, when I wrote to you (I do not know, have no idea, how many times I read it then, but I *read* it) I have never again read it (maybe paragraphs here and there) and yet I now realize, at this instant, that my whole book on Ulysses—the underlying immense gratification over what I took it to say, was, a rewording of the idea I had absorbed so deeply from *Call Me Ishmael*—it seems to me that I learned it all at once—right there—and now I understand why I have always felt a deep joy in what I felt to be the Americanism of my book—a kind of gift back to Joyce—which I now would call ours—the response which we make to the openness.

So again it is thank you, thank you.

Frances

115

Gloucester to Lawrenceville
4 November 1967 (postmark)

Frances—

Just so you have something immediately to tide you over

—& with a *3rd* book done what about immediately seeking a Guggenheim? I'll write, & you must have Joyce-persons (no?) who will now really speak up

—or do you so still despise those troughs?

Love

Charles

And don't hesitate if $50 holds the line when things get tough

116

Gloucester to Lawrenceville
4 November 1967 (postmark)

[on envelope][15]

Have a later book just in from England to send you but can't lay my hands on it in present debris

Love—O

This is just a *jeu*

15 The envelope contained the Asphodel Book Shop catalogue 13, which printed Olson's poem "The Winter the *Gen. Starks* was stuck" (*Maximus Poems*, p. 480). The "later book" would be '*West*', sent with letter no. 119 (15 November 1967).

117

Lawrenceville to Gloucester
6 November 1967

Monday 6th

Charles—

Falling over at your generosity—at moment my heart is so squeezed I can feel not very clearly, only aware very generous of you.

Here are my circumstances as to book.[16] I gave into hands of very young printer $1000 cash, all I had from sales of paperback, before I had any hint about losing my job. When disaster struck, I called him to my house and told him I don't know where money is to come from, but it must come from somewhere—however he is free to give me back job. He said no he would trust me. However, that does not relieve the terrible mental pressure I am under as to what the hell I am going to do. Job will cost 4800 without the binding. Not having a job makes it deucedly difficult for me to borrow. At the moment of course impossible. Twice in my life I have gone to Guggenheim, both times with total failure. Never raised slightest spark. Also the only man who was really in my corner became so furious at me, he had his telephone taken out and an unlisted put in so that I couldn't possibly communicate. All over something that was just the lack of being impressed about a literary item, anyway, thus tis. I do not believe there is a soul in the world who would speak up for me among whoever is supposed to be official.

At the moment 2 chapters have been set, there are a total of six. I adore my printer,[17] who is very young, because he just used his head and figured out a way to do something the manufacturer of the fotosetting machine

16 *Hermes to His Son Thoth.*

17 Boldereff was so impressed with the ingenuity and meticulousness of Edward A. Krupa Jr. and Stanley J. Kuliczkowski, the typesetters who worked on the book, that she profiled them, instead of herself, on the dust jacket flap, including a photograph of each of them.

had said couldn't be done. Thus knocking the hell out of the cost and making a 24,000 job into one for 5000. Also he did something else I love—he hunted all through the schools of Trenton and found a young negro who had nothing but desire to recommend him and he had set him to typesetting my book and the boy is doing an incredible job and I do not believe I have ever seen more difficult stuff. You will see when you see the stuff—quotes, thousands of them out of Joyce. Anyway it delights my soul, this complete mesh between three people so off the beaten track—the printer has never done a real book before in his life.

My heart beats so hard that I can hardly live through it but one of these days I will either be saved or executed or something—I can't keep hanging over an abyss the way I am now. Anyway, I am dying to get to you—as soon as this book is ready to run I am going into a complete Olson study. I'm a stubborn babe, but honest.

And no more "Kiss Kiss" business![18]

La Motz

18 Boldereff's reference to "Kiss Kiss" is not at present elucidated.

118

Gloucester to Lawrenceville
13 November 1967 (postmark 14 November 1967)

Monday November 13th

Frances,

One thing occurred to me. Had you thought of selling ahead of time? Wldn't say Barnes & Noble for example be a possible buyer of enough advance copies to give you another leg up on your printer? (I'm sure you know way more than I do about book merchandising but this fact, that Barnes & Noble had handled *Reading Finnegans Wake* seemed to me this morning possibly to be a gleam of help (?

Also to enclose to you something I only recently received myself—from whom I can't for the life of me remember, and though I've had it on my kitchen door I'd rather you had it if you want it. Otherwise heave it,[19]

love

O

19 In her next letter, Boldereff expresses gratitude for receiving the "Irish piece"—a broadside of the 1916 proclamation by the Provisional Government of the Irish Republic to the People of Ireland.

119

Gloucester to Lawrenceville
15 November 1967 (postmark 19 November 1967)

Frances—

Really crazily going along. But want you to have the other of the only two copies I guess now exist (on this side of the ocean) of a very small book of 5 poems—or maybe 6—which were published London this past year.[20] (They are re-doing it now, I understand—& will release it here through some new distributor named Grossman!

love & hope no trepidations
of any sort bother your
days or your nights—

Your Ancient & Always

Lover Charles

November 15th—a good day, & the first snow all calm and still untouched out the window. I am house-bound with an old fashioned *cold*.

[on envelope]

Frances: This was written & packaged some days ago (before your letter in yesterday, Saturday). But I haven't been out. Nor is this meant to answer your request. Charles

20 Olson enclosed a copy of '*West*' (London: Goliard, 1966), which is archived with the Frances Boldereff Papers, Archives and Special Collections, University of Connecticut, Storrs.

120

Lawrenceville to Gloucester
[16 November 1967]

Thursday

Charles dear—

I am very thrilled to have the Irish piece—never saw it before—I love Padraic Pearse and at the moment I am keeping it in a *Viking Antiquities in Ireland* which I feel an appropriate place—if ever I get my hands on some cash will have it framed—designed already in my mind.[21]

My life so incredibly horrible—hope something moves the ice jam soon—

My printer goes along with me—and neither of us knows any thing whatsoever of the future. He told me Saturday night that the man who is setting my book goes to night school at Rider and in the course he is taking my book is compulsory reading—didn't know they had even heard of Joyce—and thought all young people probably hated my book on general principles[22]—

I read through the three big Maximus books one right after another—found it all very clear and direct to me—possibly my study of Paul Klee's painting has quickened my perceptive power—What are you doing now? Can I see anything?

Françoise

21 The "Irish piece" is a broadside of the 1916 proclamation by the Provisional Government of the Irish Republic to the People of Ireland. One of the signees was Pádraic Pearse.

22 Presumably her *Reading Finnegans Wake* is being referred to.

POBLACHT NA H EIREANN.

THE PROVISIONAL GOVERNMENT

OF THE

IRISH REPUBLIC

TO THE PEOPLE OF IRELAND.

IRISHMEN AND IRISHWOMEN: In the name of God and of the dead generations from which she receives her old tradition of nationhood, Ireland, through us, summons her children to her flag and strikes for her freedom.

Having organised and trained her manhood through her secret revolutionary organisation, the Irish Republican Brotherhood, and through her open military organisations, the Irish Volunteers and the Irish Citizen Army, having patiently perfected her discipline, having resolutely waited for the right moment to reveal itself, she now seizes that moment, and, supported by her exiled children in America and by gallant allies in Europe, but relying in the first on her own strength, she strikes in full confidence of victory.

We declare the right of the people of Ireland to the ownership of Ireland, and to the unfettered control of Irish destinies, to be sovereign and indefeasible. The long usurpation of that right by a foreign people and government has not extinguished the right, nor can it ever be extinguished except by the destruction of the Irish people. In every generation the Irish people have asserted their right to national freedom and sovereignty: six times during the past three hundred years they have asserted it in arms. Standing on that fundamental right and again asserting it in arms in the face of the world, we hereby proclaim the Irish Republic as a Sovereign Independent State, and we pledge our lives and the lives of our comrades-in-arms to the cause of its freedom, of its welfare, and of its exaltation among the nations.

The Irish Republic is entitled to, and hereby claims, the allegiance of every Irishman and Irishwoman. The Republic guarantees religious and civil liberty, equal rights and equal opportunities to all its citizens, and declares its resolve to pursue the happiness and prosperity of the whole nation and of all its parts, cherishing all the children of the nation equally, and oblivious of the differences carefully fostered by an alien government, which have divided a minority from the majority in the past.

Until our arms have brought the opportune moment for the establishment of a permanent National Government, representative of the whole people of Ireland and elected by the suffrages of all her men and women, the Provisional Government, hereby constituted, will administer the civil and military affairs of the Republic in trust for the people.

We place the cause of the Irish Republic under the protection of the Most High God, Whose blessing we invoke upon our arms, and we pray that no one who serves that cause will dishonour it by cowardice, inhumanity, or rapine. In this supreme hour the Irish nation must, by its valour and discipline and by the readiness of its children to sacrifice themselves for the common good, prove itself worthy of the august destiny to which it is called.

Signed on Behalf of the Provisional Government,

THOMAS J. CLARKE.

SEAN Mac DIARMADA. THOMAS MacDONAGH.

P. H. PEARSE. EAMONN CEANNT.

JAMES CONNOLLY. JOSEPH PLUNKETT.

The Provisional Government of the Irish Republic to the People of Ireland, broadside—the "Irish piece" Boldereff refers to in letter no. 120 (16 November 1967)

121

Lawrenceville to Gloucester
29 November 1967 (postmark 29 November 1967)

Wednesday

Charles dear—

I went home for Thanksgiving and going over the mountains on the train saw snow and ice and was reminded that outside your window had also been snow—which, even with a bad cold, would be pleasant to contemplate—

I received *West*—very beautifully done—

In it there is a gem—why you have permitted it in surroundings that appear to me to be less than congenial I do not understand—at any rate this is a request to place it in some collection of your best things as I think it one of the best in anyone's writing—*Psyche*. It reminds of Paul Klee's painting and I, who worship Paul Klee, can not praise higher.

Grossman, in this smallest of worlds, is a client of my lawyer and the person I was vaguely considering asking to handle *A Blakean Translation*, but then I hit on a better thing, doing it myself—and how very glad I am as I am positive no other publisher would have put the push behind selling it that the man who worked for me did and of course no one else would have allowed me to keep all of what I earned—which is where I got what I have put into the new book as you know—Grossman seems to be young and bright, but my guess is the day has already passed for anyone new coming into much—there is only possible today either the biggies or to do what I do and the amazing thing is, what a very large amount of absolutely independent publishing is being done—that's what thrilled me about the catalogue you sent me and I have seen and heard of much else in places like the New York Public and in persons as established as Ellsworth Mason publishing a small Joyce item on his own. All delights me—it proves that under the heavy weight of the dying capitalistic world, how much life there is in America.

I am going forward totally on the blind, as when you first knew me—knowing nothing about where my bread and shelter are to come from—anyway I am trying to make a rather huge shift in my existence—

I saw a piece of Italian metal sculpture at the International in Pittsburgh which I loved—a group of sort of poppy flower forms standing about 1 ½–2 feet high with modern and unrecognizable but beautiful forms and rather thick stems and underneath apples of various sizes lying around—the grouping was just sheer beauty and I would adore to have it in or near my place in Woodward—no one else seemed specially impressed—it had not been sold and had won no award nor mention—American people not particularly sensitive.

Also the flower show in Pittsburgh is a very real work of art—nothing but flowers, in the lovely old Phipps Conservatory to which the city is adding a new, very modern and sensitively very right, entrance—heavy stone and concrete roof but whoever did it knew what he was about because it goes perfectly with the rather delicate glass structure behind it—

Maybe *Psyche* and the metal art should be somewhere side by side.

Frances

I am so thrilled to see this year go by you can have no idea—every minute of it has been torture. I see it is already almost gone and psychically I am just pushing those days off as fast as I can, a physical sensation.

122

Gloucester to Lawrenceville
2 December 1967 (postmark 4 December 1967)

Saturday December 2nd

Frances

It's really marvelous (certainly murderous) that you shld pick out of the two poems in West which are not my own one of them which if you will look again are two of Drummond Hadley's whom I there "publish" for the first time. So at least we show the same taste at least, at least in *that* instance. Though God knows taste is certainly nothing an artist can at all often care about (*afford*) and better in fact avoid if he is doing (going to do) what he best figure he damn well does do (best does).

OK. Sorry the rest was so uncongenial to you! Lordy me

your own

Charles

PS That *is* a freeze-out

Just to cheer you up (*to make you feel better*) (—possibly!) I send you another from another book now in preparation.[23]

23 What poem Olson enclosed is not known. At this time *Maximus Poems IV, V, VI* was being typeset for Cape Goliard, London.

123

Gloucester to Lawrenceville
6 December 1967 (postmark)

[This envelope contains only an order form
from University of Washington Press announcing
*The Ireland of Sir Jonah Barrington:
Selections from his Personal Sketches*,
ed. Hugh B. Staples.]

124

Lawrenceville to Gloucester
7 December 1967 (postmark 7 December 1967)

Thursday—

Charles dear—

Can scarcely imagine anything more total than what I sent—if such a blow fell to me I can imagine how would feel the ice forming—anyway—I am very happy in my heart that you should have been so generous towards another, as only the great in spirit are and as you told me long ago, one of the few things a poet *must* be. I will only say that although his name was clearly above it such a construction of his name's being there would never have entered my head and whether that be typography or stupidity I can not say—the modern form making the wide jumps it does I thought the name as part of the total poem, as there are other (recognizable) names therein—I simply construed it as an inclusion to achieve a total atmosphere.

Your new poem ties in with something I am working on very slowly in my own mind—and if I can find the right passage will quote you out of a woman whom I admire and whose obscurity seems to be total—I hunted for her book and found it in Princeton University Library—where it had sat since 1929—close to 40 years—no one having ever taken it out before me—I have been trying to find a copy to buy but so far unsuccessful. Dora Marsden—*The Definition of the Godhead*.

I am going to type out for you a few pages[24]—it is thrilling to me that you should express in a poem an entire subject matter which completely thrills me and which I feel is of the essence of a new break-through in our time. Oh Charles, Charles—the times without number we have found ourselves tossing back and forth the same ball—the quick of the universe.

Frances

24 These typed pages are missing, as is the poem Boldereff refers to.

125

Lawrenceville to Gloucester (postcard)
13 December 1967 (postmark)

Remember the night in Woodward when the 3 of us walked home from the restaurant in snow so thick we couldn't see one another?

Frances

126

Gloucester to Lawrenceville
15 December 1967 (postmark 16 December 1967)

Friday (a.m.)
December 15th

Frances,

Actually, you started so many things with your letter I've been busy all week trying to run around them. —And haven't yet finished.

So this is solely to acknowledge it and to say I'll be back with more again soon. Or at least write you freely without the interest your own letter, & the Marsden quote, have involved me in.

Charles

127

Gloucester to Lawrenceville
29 December 1967 (postmark 30 December 1967)

Frances—Hope you are all right. Appreciated your card (have never, of course, forgotten that walk, single-file, down that highway of the three of us.

Have been somewhat delayed in reaching you sooner due to two blocked *ears* (one week of, and very irritating: it is like losing one's spiritual hands. All activity is off.

Let me hear from you.   Charles   December 29th
(1967)

PS: haven't yet, curiously, been quite able to get NU(*-UN*) off mind. At same time of such importance do I regard "negative" anyway as the secret of analogy that I also can't relieve the occupation by (of) it by writing anything, either to you or of it. Which though can be of course good sign of weather, likewise.

128

Lawrenceville to Gloucester
6 January 1968

Saturday Jan 6

Charles dear—

I never heard of what is wrong with your ears—but hope you are in the care of a reliable person, as the ear is very close to the brain and dangerous to fool around with—I hope it is gone away, whatever caused it and that you are feeling more human again.

I have been through the most intensely nervous period of my life—in fact, began to shake like a really old lady—but now, thank God, my plans have begun to jell and while very far from knowing where and how I am to provide for myself physically, nevertheless I feel inside that the corner has been turned and my year (exactly one year today since I was fired) of agony over.[25] On Wednesday I went down to Rutgers and registered to take a Master's in Library Service—and after I get the degree—planning to work in a college library—

On Friday my unemployment compensation came to an end and it will be three weeks before I will hear from the bank to whom I applied for a government student loan; the man I finally got to at the university, after being there all day and receiving an amazing variety of rebuffs, was kindness itself and said that if the gov't thing did not come through to come back to see him and he will arrange some deferred payment—however, and good as that is and pleased as I am—still need actual money to live on—but believe me I will batter on the doors till I find some kind of answer—

The whole thing from the first glimmering of the idea to now has been one of immense suffering—I have been doublecrossed and insulted and

25 Olson wrote in the margin, "Impossible?" In her letter of 1 November 1967 (no. 113), Boldereff had indicated that she had just been fired.

frustrated—so I feel sly and immensely victorious to have finally maneuvered my actual registration—for once I get the degree I can work almost anywhere I want—including Woodward. My secret hope is to work around here until I can borrow enough cash to make Woodward into a livable house—and once it is ready—then to go back at last—and live among my trees and woods which I so much love and at least be home every weekend if not every day.

The terrible desire there is in this country to prevent anyone from finding a strong, good answer, if he does not subscribe to the general slavery, I do not have to describe to you—I can only tell you I have never been so terribly harassed so constantly, for so long—and I feel like the King of the world—no matter what happens from now on—to have gotten what I wanted, with the combined forces of everyone turned away in an opposite direction. (No one kept their promises to me—perfect record of non-cooperation.) When I was very young I always knew, in a very deep way, that there is only one thing in the world one can put one's foot on, and that is, one's own accomplishment—and in this endeavor—what brought me through was just that—my A average at U. of Michigan and my two books which Rutgers has in their library and uses in their graduate English department.

I have applied for so many jobs it is unbelievable—and at some little moment—like a breeze across my face—I realized I had taken the last insult I intended to endure.

Your girl—

Françoise

129

Gloucester to Lawrenceville
9 January 1968 (postmark 10 January 1968)

Frances! How wonderful to hear from you Tuesday January 9th (marvelous Post Office—Trenton, New Jersey, to Gloucester, Massachusetts PM 6 Jan to Jan 9th!): CP Snow sd when post office & railroad conductors decline the civilization has!

& to learn you are now *on your own road* that employment way too

I don't know what my own future holds, and these have been desperate days—(you can't imagine, I shldn't think, what an *impossible* effort it is for a man like myself, finally *compulsive*, to live alone & try to keep up housekeeping etc—God almost 4 years of it, & I am strained beyond endurance—and Sunday (with my two children visiting me alone here!

And yesterday the equivalent of *40 below*, the oil man today tells me the unbelievable winds plus the temperature itself—*14 below*: I thought surely the *chance* that a farther turn & the earth wld have spun into that science fictory fiction or historical future hanging over I suppose kids' minds (I never myself conjured it up until literally yesterday—

I was so fearful, not hearing from you, you might actually be in misery I'd have called you last night had I not hated telephones so much.

In any case let me again lay 100 on you for these few more days before you do start the ball rolling—& all love for you from me, & utter congratulations on your decision: it gives me myself sight just when I need it (having turned aside to these things of my own life—& to my utter astonishment I discover that at 57 (I was that 2 weeks ago tomorrow!) God help us but old age does suddenly stare one in the face! I hate it of course,

love,

Charles

130

Lawrenceville to Gloucester
16 January 1968 (postmark 16 January 1968)[26]

Tuesday—Jan 16

Charles dear—

I am sorry not to have written at once—and it is a good thing you put it so far inside—had it been right there I would have sat down and returned it; reading the letter and pondering over your words, by the time I came to the check I was *very* surprised and very grateful. I have been waiting to hear from many different sources, but realized today I can not wait any longer to let you know that I received your check and how very generous and loving of you (uncertain for your own future) it was to send it.

For a long time your children have been tugging at my heart strings—I have hesitated ever to say anything—so very uncertain over my own physical capacity and security—but I would like to say that in the summer time I expect a lull of a few weeks (I am going to school in the summer also, but there is a period when they *do* shut down I feel sure) and if you would care to send your two children to me, I should be delighted to have them—if they like me and all goes well then I could think about later on. You see I am going through all this terrible effort because I want to work near my home and I have such a job promised—so after going through all kinds of hell I would hate like the devil to throw it all away, just as the plan began to work.

26 This envelope is archived at Storrs with a handwritten note by Olson:

My 9th body began this year Duncan tells me and in doing so gives light to me, song to give me too from himself in having *horloge*

49 (7 × 7)

57 (8 × 7: 56

now the live of 9 × 7 is 63

now the 1st of my *9th* body

I start on Monday—due to the NY bus omitting New Brunswick on its early runs I have to get up at 6:30 and stand outside for NY bus to go only to Princeton and there wait 20 more minutes for local to New Brunswick, so I expect to be a little bit weary the first few weeks, until I get used to it.

I can certainly realize how ghastly it is for you to take care of yourself and I would not mind doing it now and then, but you know how terribly I loathe housekeeping and cooking and when I am here alone it is possible for various reasons for me to sidestep an awful lot of it. Besides when you live alone you are only obligated to yourself and having worked like a demon for the Lord knows how many years—I am very loathe to commit myself to *any* obligation. We *should* have that darling double house up in Laurelton we used to see and love![27]

Anyway I am very very curious as to what will happen about my book—I can easily envisage a rather spectacular failure—will be glad when I have it in my hand and have sold enough to pay the printer—after that, I don't care at all—sent to a professor in Princeton last week to request an opportunity to read his paper on acceleration of cosmic rays[28]—he sent it to me—and lord! how interesting it is—we at last really live in that unfolding infinite world old Bruno was always talking about. I adore Bruno. I am expecting to see him fully translated as a result of my book—at least I am fervently praying!

Just discovered I am in a very nasty situation about delivery of oil to my house—I have been billed for oil put in my landlord's tank and since it has been done over a fairly long period, on purpose, it's going to be a messy thing all round! Great age we live in—

Is your house warm? The terrible storm in Scotland may have been part of what was making Gloucester so frightfully cold—Let me know how you are—Lucinda sends her regards.

Frances

27 Laurelton is a village near Woodward, Pennsylvania.

28 Whom Boldereff contacted at Princeton is unknown.

131

Gloucester to Lawrenceville
19 January 1968 (postmark 23 January 1968)

Frances,

This will at least greet you about when you start that schedule, which like so much else in this nation has gotten so cruel to the individual—and at the same time mark completely my respect for you in what you are undertaking.—I had in fact just been quoting from your previous letter (to a 15 year old high school sophomore who came to see me today for the 1st time—who was all-A's herself last year, and is a dancer or proposes to be one) when, since, I have read your last letter. And of course know all you do mean (the more so now that I too have had to become my own housekeeper! Lord what a work it is! And how absolutely the young have only respect for the single accomplishment. At the same time that the society, the one we lived current with, has finally squeezed us out—almost! Not quite. And so Frances go ahead without any worry that vicious as it is around there are voices etc. Or ears. And eyes, beautiful eyes again among at least the kids.

(And like you say beautiful work being done: you introduced me to Kramer maybe 20 years ago! I still carry that paquette (paquet!) of his, sent to you, around as one of my holy goods.

Solely to wish you well in what I'm sure is a rough one,

Yrs
lovingly
Charles

Friday January 19th 'LXVIII

PS As of my own children, let's leave it out ahead at the same time I love the idea actually—more, in fact, of driving them myself, someday, to visit you at Woodward. That certainly makes sense. As they are their summers get all planned out before I am anywhere, Kate's because she is now of course old enough to be almost on her own (and will in fact this summer go to school with her step-father!),[29] and Charles Peter because he's an athlete, and 12, and therefore has *his* schedule, of Little League baseball etc. They did, last summer, for the 1st time since Bet's death, spend time together (in Maine, with Connie, and though Charles Peter had to be flown from the island because of an eye-tooth which never came down, & suddenly therefore I now am faced with $800 worth of this new thing orthodontry (! it sounds like a substitute for orthodox!)—Actually if I wrote you I had the two of them here two weeks ago, that *too* was *1st* time I've had them together under my own roof—& that mind you, for one day!—in likewise going on 4 years! So it both wld & yet wld be something to accomplish to have them visit you.

The best thing really wld, when we ourselves do make it, is to just drive & see you soon sometime, on a, like, lark. (As I wanted myself, last summer, to come to see you—I was then in Ohio—when you were in Woodward. But yr own vacations are so much your own used privacies too that you well better plan them as you have for yourself alone. I *hope* Lucinda will take my very best love through you. Send it anyway (assuming she still is in Seattle?

Love altogether, and don't of course despair. And call on me if anything should get too much. Yours, so much, Charles

(In rereading this I see the handwriting is *most* difficult. Read as much of it as you choose—& don't please mind: it is better I write now, while I can, I want so much to, than wait. Yrs me.)

29 In September 1959 Connie had married George Bunker, who was dean at the Philadelphia College of Art.

132

Trenton to Gloucester
4 February 1968 (postmark)

Sunday

Charles dear—

My time is eaten into in a way I find hard to realize—the three days at school of course are full—I have four days not at school—they give such an enormous amount of outside reading that it is literally swamping me—compounded by the fact that so far I have not been able to find most of the books anywhere I can borrow and I live not terribly near to any library so I have, for instance, today to go to New Brunswick and study all afternoon and tonight have a date with my printer—

I like going to school, although there is much about it which I intensely do not go along with—for instance, in all classes but one, the students do the large part of the talking—I consider that a gyp, since I haven't the slightest interest in what goes on in another student's mind—also the enormous amount of reading in books one finds it practically impossible to relate to—there is lots of verbiage going on in this here country—and by deepest instinct I distrust *talk*. However, I am interested in my professors, not because they appeal to me, but because they are so different from one another and I have one whom I really like—a young, second-generation Italian from Springfield, Mass., who is a political scientist and has been, or is in, government somewhere—he has a passionate desire to see the unliterate brought into libraries—the people who have never been in libraries and to whom they do not come natural—and I feel the same way—if the libraries don't do it, who will?—so he has put an idea in my head—

I had no idea your children were so old and of course I get the picture very clearly—

And of course you have to come either to Woodward or here to visit me—I don't understand what you mean about Woodward last year because last year (1967) I didn't get to Woodward except for one day—I believe less than 24 hours—just to do a much needed rescue job in my tiny orchard—I had to unwrap by hand the prongs of basket weave steel fencing—6 feet high and rewrap it into longer pieces—in the drizzling rain—sat out there all day, my fingers getting sorer and sorer, prongs like that, each single one to be woven into the other so as to hold together—also I had to *unwrap* the fences as they were—all too small and the trees had no way to grow—anyway I finished it and came home feeling like the old woman who lived in the shoe—

I am applying for Social Security—no idea how much I will get, but at the present no other source of income—I hear it takes about 3 months to get under way—anyway at the moment I have the gov't loan and when it comes time to pay tuition, if situation looks bad I will ask the university's permission to pay after I graduate.

I have already pulled a boo-boo by talking about the asst-dean who is one of my teachers to another pupil and I am sure conversation was reported back to her—she is angry and hurt—so that is a pure Motz phenomenon which comes from my highly critical and outspoken approach to life—one father, one twin and I have all ruined our success in life by being so fiery—

It isn't possible for me these days to carry on a correspondence—I also have the feeling you do not like to write letters—so when you have something to show me and a book you promised—I forget where and what but remember you said there was something in works you wanted me to have—send it—not that I don't want to hear from you—I do—but I am really pressed by this studying—it looks like a fantastically busy year right up to the day you get your degree.

I now understand how hopeless engineers, dentists, etc etc feel about reading—they are so fantastically bogged down by the enormous flow of data in their own field—what I object to about what I am reading is that lots of it I simply can not lock with—it absolutely refuses to sink in—but we are supposed to discuss what we read in class. The system goes very deeply into me—I probably hate it as much as any student in the U.S.—I so very much want to be taught and not to hear students talking—I always get into trouble when I talk and yet we are supposed to—and already, not that I care, but I can feel how much most of the students do not like me—my mind is such a different kind and something about me that rubs fur the wrong way of all middle-class people—of course, I am glad—since they rub my fur the wrong way—but in a school today—like Rutgers—hard going for my type—

Frances

The envelope is one I happen to have—it doesn't mean anything.[30]

30 It is an envelope belonging to her previous employer, D. Van Nostrand Company, Inc.

133

Lawrenceville to Gloucester
2 March 1968 (postmark)

Charles dear—

In greatest haste—PO is going to close—

I am aghast at letter I wrote you—amazing that one could write something so far from any desire—it only meant to say I am so busy I am going nuts—not in a position to carry on a regular correspondence but term comes to an end around middle of May I think—would love to see you—anyway never meant to imply I don't want to *hear* only I can not do anything now—library school work *fantastic* in volume—nutty—

Frances

Letters have genius for misrepresenting feelings

134

Gloucester to Lawrenceville
12 March 1968 (Boston postmark 25 March 1968)

March 12th

Frances,

Don't mind at all, that I have been so silent.[31] (I have all I can do, keeping up with work, and house-work, to make it at all—and it is regrettable to me that I can't see you, or hear from you or myself write to you more often.)

I hope everything *financially* at least does now go more smoothly—and that the boringness of the preparation to be a librarian also only bothers you now with the end in sight.

Love, and please write if you want to take a breath—

Yrs, faithfully,
Charles

31 Although he does not mention it, Olson had been looking at Boldereff's *A Blakean Translation of Joyce's Circe*; on page 47 he dates a marginal note 6 February 1968.

135

Lawrenceville to Gloucester[32]
9 April 1968 (postmark 9 April 1968)

Tuesday, April 9

Charles dear—

Today we had no classes because of King's funeral, but I did not know this and so went to New Brunswick where I met other students who also did not know—(evidently no coordination of an effort to inform) and since I was there, decided to stay and study, since I have done no homework for two weeks because of exams and projects I have to work on—so worked all morning and part of afternoon—I understand my classes will be over the middle of May—and summer school does not start until July—I am working very hard on my book because I am fearful about the money situation (international) and want to get my book out before the international market collapses.

The school is so boring and so meaningless it is shocking to me—but I guess not much different from other fields of study—Marshall McLuhan strikes me as being a most consummate knave—E. Toerge gave it to me as a gift—she thinks he's great—

He misinterprets everything, but is giving sly warnings to us all—

At the moment I am hoping just to get through the school—and get the piece of paper—which I want I guess I told you because I want to make Woodward more comfortable and more space—so that I can live there permanently. That is my last "desire" and after that I hope to stop working and just enjoy life. At the moment I am engaged on a search concerning Marlowe, T. Watson[33] and Bruno—which excites me, as I love

32 The letter was forwarded to San Francisco, c/o Donald M. Allen, whom Olson was visiting.

33 Presumably sixteenth-century English poet Thomas Watson. See Boldereff's dedication in *Hermes to His Son Thoth*.

them all three dearly—I have sent for a Ph.D. to the people in Ann Arbor—and I *wish* they would hurry!

The financing of my book is still an unknown quantity, but I received a large sum from S.S. and am applying it all to the book—exactly how all will come out in the end I have no remote idea—it is inconceivable to me that it could flop entirely—however, I am hoping to sell enough to pay the printer. Summer school should be over early in August—maybe we could make a plan to meet between then and the Fall semester—let me know what you think.

I love Marlowe and Watson and Bruno—they delight my soul to the very core—funny how Watson has completely disappeared—Watson *loved* Chaucer and wanted to bring back good old words into use. I have invited a very young friend to supper—

I hope the spring sunshine makes you happy—

Frances

136

Gloucester to Lawrenceville
1 July 1968 (postmark 2 July 1968)

July 1st

Frances,

Simply, to catch us up: though I am now well (and better than I have been in, like, *years*—I hope) I had a wretched trip from late March on, 1st to Beloit, in Wisconsin, then in San Francisco, ill but working (on television, no less: that is, the future of it, and enough to stay away from!), a couple of weeks longer there dipping my fingers into the politics of the present; ending Tucson, for two weeks (with my friend Hadley, the poet, & his wife & 3 babies—all *under* 3!)

I returned here for Charles Peter's birthday (May 12th) & thereafter continued so poorly I ended up in the hospital (for two weeks & $1000!) & am still in three doctors' care! And attentions, actually useful.

Since, plus, I have been busy (with staff, no less etc—including now housekeepers, & soon, possibly, a secretary—no less!

But I do excuse myself for such a long silence, particularly with yourself in that library chute—so please let me hear how you are, how it did go, and what was your free time this summer (on the chance we can see each other—

Love,
Charles

Also: any of your news on those more important matters you are busy with: the book etc.

137

Lawrenceville to Gloucester
6 July 1968 (postmark 6 July 1968)

July 6

Charles dear—

I hope your chest has not been the reason you were in the hospital—what is the cause—and are you cured? I hate to think of you as feeling wretched.

I hated library school so violently it affected my health—what a farce and a lie and how disgusting it is—all toadies—all purveyors of the capitalists' clamor—let's do away with books—old fashioned detestable items and let us get on with the "implosion of knowledge" more TV, more videotape, more computers, more pupils—and the knave supreme among them all—Marshall McLuhan, whom I am supposed to read.

I am now taking a course in AV and the woman who teaches it is a darling, so I find the course the most pleasant so far—she tells you things very clearly and you understand what she is saying—my courses in systems analysis, administration, readers' services are all garbage, confusion reigns supreme, but yet you are supposed to untangle this garbage and write long lucid answers to very difficult questions on the exams—it is *very difficult*, that's what's so maddening—it is so hard you study yourself sick and at the same time you learn absolutely nothing—neither technique, nor theory nor any solid subject matter—Books are as passé as a literal reading of the Biblical age of man—

I will be free in September until the 11th—I have to start classes on the 12th and I was going to go to Woodward but it has just occurred to me I promised to work in a library starting Sept 1 and I need the money desperately as I do not have enough to finish out my year of schooling—I will try to see the man early next week—I am sure I could work out a few days—can you get a car? The food in the Inn is so horrible I can not eat it and there is nowhere else to go there so I drive all the way to Lewisburg (21 miles) to eat where there is a marvelous Inn with really delicious food—If you could go to Woodward any time between 3rd and 11th let me know—I will see what I can do about my schedule—or would it suit you better to come here—if you could come here there wouldn't be any problem—also if you cared to have me (since I sleep on the floor and do not need a bedroom) I would be willing to come to Gloucester. Let me know which would be best and *exactly* because I have to agree to work certain definite nights in the library—

My book was delivered to me two days ago—I owe somewhere between 3700–4000—plus what I already poured into it—I am sending you a copy and all I can say is—it cost me everything.[34] I spent literally months of going to bed every night with a heart pounding so hard I always thought there would not be any next day. I pulled it out of nowhere—because not one person wanted to help me and to try to figure out a way was a sheer medieval contest of will which went on so long I finally came to a breaking point—and after that I can't remember except that somehow the printer and I agreed to go on and I received a small amount of help—I feel as though I am united by an effort spiritually as great as Joyce's in forcing the thing into existence with everyone's back turned against me—I hope you will find a few sentences that will interest you. The hard part is you see I do not believe there is anything in it to make anyone *want* it—it preaches no doctrine, it has no either good or bad rallying points—it isn't juicy—it covers no subject anyone is interested in—no dreams, no Freud, no glorious comments of a general nature—just a very hard working dig job on what the master said—and he said he wanted Ireland to stop being a fool and who cares about Ireland?

I hope you will approve of the physical aspects.

And I hope you are all better—please let me know how your chest is.

You will understand what it cost me and that helps me—

Ever and as always with my love

Frances

34 Olson's copy of *Hermes to His Son Thoth* (at Storrs) is inscribed: "For Charles—what came out of the Woodward nights. Frances."

138

Gloucester to Lawrenceville (telegram)
[10 July 1968]

FRANCES BOLDEREFF

19 HENDRICKSON RD LAWRENCEVILLE NJER

YOU HAVE A RIGHT TO BE EXTREMELY HAPPY I SEE WHY IT COSTS SO MUCH IT IS AS THOUGH YOU HAD DONE IT YOURSELF JUST TO GET YOU FIRST WORD LOVE

CHARLES

139

Gloucester to Lawrenceville
10 July 1968 (postmark 11 July 1968)

Wednesday

Frances,

Without even reading further—just looking, will you have your people send 5 of your book to the following (& put inside each the proper envelope?

Robert Duncan, care of the summer session,
Department of English, State University of
New York at Buffalo, Annex A, Main Street
& Bailey, Buffalo New York

Jack Clarke
149 College Street
Buffalo New York

Gerrit Lansing
475 Washington Street
Gloucester Massachusetts

Zoe & Bill Brown and Thorpe
Bolinas, California

Robert Kelly and his
Annadale-on-the-Hudson,
New York

Love
Charles

140

Gloucester to Lawrenceville
11 July 1968 (postmark)

West Gloucester

____________________ Condylura
cristata
on Atlantic
Street West
Gloucester
spinning on its
star-wheel
nose,
in the middle of the
tarvia,

probably because it had been
knocked in the head (was
actually fighting all the time,
with its fore-paws at
the lovely mushroom growth
of its nose, snow-ball flake pink flesh
of a gentian, until I
took an oar out of the back seat of the station
\ wagon
and removed it
like a pea on a knife to
the side of the road

stopped its dance dizzy dance,
on its own nose out of its head
working as though it would get rid of
its own pink appendage

like a flower dizzy
with its own self

like the prettiest thing in the world drilling
itself into the

pavement

and I gave it, I hope, all the marshes of Walker's Creek

to get it off what might also seem
what was wrong with it, that the highway
had magnetized the poor thing

the loveliest animal I believe I ever did see
In such a quandary

and off the marshes
of Walker's Creek fall
graduatedly so softly to
the Creek and the Creek to
Ipswich Bay an arm
of the Atlantic Ocean

send the Star Nosed Mole
all into the grass
all away from the dizzying
highway if that was what was wrong

with the little thing, spinning
in the middle of the
highway

(appeared in *F... Y...* , *A Magazine of the Arts*, New York, edited by Ed Sanders, as the "God" issue, December 1964)[35]

[on envelope]

Pardon the condition of the enclosed—but you asked for it, handsomely, some long time ago

35 Olson was enclosing a photocopy of the poem from *Fuck You, A Magazine of the Arts* 5, no. 7 (August 1964): pp. 8–9.

141

Lawrenceville to Gloucester
14 July 1968 (postmark)

Saturday night

Charles dear—

I think the poem is a lovely thing—it touches me in some deep place—the delicate tentacles of reach from Olson to Woodward to Lucinda to her mother make it also seem to me the most tender and exquisite of love poems—it makes me feel like Joyce's "kissmiss"—the closing of the perfect circle of touch—I am delighted and will copy it out for Lucinda who will also love it although she carefully avoids all of her mother's enthusiasms. I will just tell her you sent it and make no comment. It would be wonderful if she were to make some lovely little drawing but I will not ask. Her drawing of Hermes Trismegistus on the title page.[36]

I am the wrapper and mailer and I will send off to your friends Monday—I am in the midst of term papers and exams therefore frightfully pressed for time—your kindness, Charles, is very right—I can imagine nothing more desirable than to have 5 sensitive people look at it—I do thank you.

I shall often think of the mole—his image is such a perfect picture of present-day frustration—in fact includes all the elements which create the special horror—including the universe.

Please tell me what your doctor *says*; what can he *do*, what can't he do?

Frances

36 See title page of *Hermes to His Son Thoth*.

142

Gloucester to Lawrenceville
31 July 1968 (postmark 1 August 1968)

Frances,

Kelly was here last night, & *may*, fairly, be an answer—had rec'd the book, & was proposing to send you poems of his own point-to-point, apparently (the 1st one at least, in his book) to your title—equally had, as he said, not yet read, though had been pleased to receive yrs.

So—equally—as of possibly the others (as well as myself!) They are all new, & persons, who wld, I was sure, be interested—& that you don't hear, immediately (or you may have: I have only had word over the fence from Lansing, & acknowledgment from the Browns (in California) but nothing from Clarke or Duncan—and that little bit, last night, from the Kelly.

OK solely to get back to you, myself—and hope the end of this dreary library training gives you by now the pleasure of its coming toward the close.

I'm working very well (it's a sweet exceptional summer here anyway; and though I have still to "behave" (the problem seems simply to be to take care to be taken care of—food & that stuff; and equally not socialize too much!

All of which, is to the good.

Love

Yrs

(Wednesday July 31st)

143

Lawrenceville to Gloucester
3 August 1968 (postmark 3 August 1968)

Saturday—Aug 3

Charles dear—

So glad to hear from you—I have been thinking about and wondering and so glad to hear that all you have to do is be careful—

I think I am going to run up to Woodward for a few days on the 12th—I have to get my place painted—otherwise it will fall apart—I will see old Davis who used to live across the street from me in State College—I know you cannot come but if you could come, I can get some old geezer up there to haul me around in a car—so you wouldn't have to do anything—
I realize you probably can't but how marvellous it would be to be there with you—

Don't worry about reading my book—I know you aren't interested and are *helping* me because of the help and not because the thing in itself means anything to you—

I think it was absolutely darling to send it to those 5 men—I am so glad to be seen by them—

For some strange reason Cornell at Ithaca has already bought and paid for 2 copies—

I am interested in some ideas which aren't connected with Joyce right now—and am waiting for a new book on physics by the man on the West Coast I admire so much—Dewey Larson—

All the life in America seems to be in the west—

Please write soon and tell me when you can come either to Woodward or to Lawrenceville—

So glad if you will get back on your feet and be strong in your chest—where all good men suffer—

I put my arms around you, sweet man.

Frances

144

Gloucester to Lawrenceville (telegram)
14 September 1968

FRANCES BOLDEREFF
19 HENDRICKSON RD LAWRENCEVILLE NJER

I'VE NOT BEEN WELL AND I BEG YOU THEREFORE TO FORGIVE BOTH MY FAILURE TO LET YOU KNOW OR TO COME PLEASE LET ME HEAR FROM YOU LOVE

CHARLES

145

Gloucester to Lawrenceville
4 November 1968 (postmark)

I'm *completely* sympathetic[37]—and they'd enjoy, the fools, making mock of you (I have, in two instances, in recent years, had to fight physically—or at least come on so, with the "young"—and the other night (two nights ago) innocently out, for dinner, on an invitation of an architect (of the Museum here, and he and his wife friends for years—plus another guest, the chief columnist of the newspaper, and an exceptional newspaperman (but, because he is also a "rival" historian now, of Gloucester)—the whole thing, it turned out, was not at all social but to bag me—Wow, I have *suffered* since.[38]

And don't, please, even though you know how very much I admire & respect your intent, on this library study, feel that boxed in: remember, you are the "Designer" the original stationery I rec'd from you said—and so *bad* has printing & book design itself become in this country (despite what *you'd* know the *commercial* field may or may not be capable of) that my own sense wld be you could as well hang out your shingle again soon—and orders, like, come in!

I hope so, and that though you have suffered in that area what I can't even guess, I *do know* small presses—or what *used* to be style presses (I'm thinking of the California bay area) have, at present, *solely* one man whom they can turn to

(I will, in fact, enclose with this, an announcement of his *last* book—and one if not the *only* one he's done of my own: things:[39] for he too has had to go to L.A. (Los Angeles), & go commercial, to support his family.

Love,

O.

37 The letter Olson refers to is missing. There are no further letters from Boldereff extant.

38 The newspaperman would be Joseph Garland and the architect Donald Monell.

39 Olson enclosed the printed announcement from Oyez Press for Ann Charters, *Olson/Melville: A Study in Affinity* (Berkeley: Oyez, 1968), "available November 30, 1968." The book was designed by Graham Mackintosh.

146

Gloucester to Lawrenceville
12 December 1968

Frances—Just a note to get this off to you[40]—& *will*, if the other—lady's book—does come in (was delayed due to Mackintosh *forgetting*, for a month, to get it to the *printer*!)—is now supposed to have been ready December 10th.[41]

The enclosed, for what you find it.

love & simply
to get business done

Charles

Thursday December 12th
(1968)

40 Olson is enclosing *Pleistocene Man: Letters to Jack Clarke* (Buffalo: Institute of Further Studies, 1968).

41 Presumably Olson later sent Boldereff the copy of Ann Charters's *Olson/Melville: A Study in Affinity*.

147

Gloucester to Lawrenceville (telegram)
3 March 1969

YOU ARE IMPOSSIBLE PLEASE LET ME KNOW HOW YOU ARE.
I AM BURIED IN SNOW LOVE
CHARLES

148

Gloucester to Lawrenceville
28 May 1969 (postmark)

My dear sweet Frances—Just in another burst of love for you (they come in such gusts my whole nature at this moment (as I write) bursts on you)

Love

Charles

PS I adore you

ACKNOWLEDGEMENTS

The editors gratefully acknowledge the assistance of Lucy Wilner and Melissa Watterworth Batt; Jenny Penberthy for reading early drafts of the introduction; and the sustaining care that Greg Gibson at Talonbooks has given to this project.

WORKS BY FRANCES BOLDEREFF

Ward, Frances. *A Primer of Morals for Medea*. Woodward, PA: Russian Classic Non-Fiction Library, 1949.

Boldereff, Frances. *To Greet You with the New Year*. Pamphlet. New York: n.p., 1953.

———. *Reading Finnegans Wake*. Woodward, PA: Classic Non-Fiction Library, 1959.

———. *A Blakean Translation of Joyce's Circe*. Woodward, PA: Classic Non-Fiction Library, 1965.

———. *Hermes to His Son Thoth: Being Joyce's Use of Giordano Bruno in Finnegans Wake*. Woodward, PA: Classic Non-Fiction Library, 1968.

Motz, Reighard (pseud.). *Time as Joyce Tells It*. Mifflinburg, PA: Mulford Colebrook, [1977].

Rose, Thomasine (pseud.). *Verbi-Voco-Visual: The Presence of Bishop Berkeley in Finnegans Wake*. The Netherlands: Bellefonte Editeur, 1981.

Phipps, Frances. *Let Me Be Los: Codebook for Finnegans Wake*. Lubbock, TX: Toth-Maatian, 1985.

Boldereff, Frances, and Charles Olson. *A Modern Correspondence*. Edited by Ralph Maud and Sharon Thesen. Middletown, CT: Wesleyan University Press, 1999.

SELECTED WORKS BY CHARLES OLSON

Call Me Ishmael. New York: Reynal and Hitchcock, 1947; New York: Grove, 1958; San Francisco: City Lights Books, 1967; London: Cape, 1967; Baltimore: Johns Hopkins University Press, 1997.

y & x. Washington, D.C.: Black Sun, 1948.

In Cold Hell, In Thicket. Dorchester, MA: Origin, 1953; San Francisco: Four Seasons, 1967.

The Maximus Poems 1–10. Stuttgart: Jonathan Williams, 1953.

Mayan Letters. Edited by Robert Creeley. Palma, Majorca: Divers, 1953; London: Cape, 1968.

The Maximus Poems 11–22. Stuttgart: Jonathan Williams, 1956.

O'Ryan 2 4 6 8 10. San Francisco: White Rabbit, 1958.

Projective Verse. New York: Totem, 1959.

The Maximus Poems. New York: Jargon / Corinth, 1960; London: Cape Goliard, 1970.

The Distances. New York: Grove, 1960; London: Evergreen, 1960.

A Bibliography on America for Ed Dorn. San Francisco: Four Seasons, 1964.

O'Ryan 12345678910. San Francisco: White Rabbit, 1965.

Proprioception. San Francisco: Four Seasons, 1965.

Human Universe and Other Essays. Edited by Donald Allen. San Francisco: Auerhahn , 1965; New York: Grove, 1967.

Selected Writings. Edited by Robert Creeley. New York: New Directions, 1966.

'West'. London: Goliard, 1966.

Maximus Poems IV, V, VI. London: Cape Goliard, 1968; New York: Grossman, 1968.

Pleistocene Man: Letters to Jack Clarke. Buffalo: Institute of Further Studies, 1968.

Letters for Origin, 1950–1956. Edited by Albert Glover. London: Cape Goliard, 1968; New York: Cape Goliard / Grossman, 1970.

Causal Mythology. San Francisco: Four Seasons, 1969.

The Special View of History. Edited by Ann Charters. Berkeley: Oyez, 1970.

Archaeologist of Morning. London: Cape Goliard, 1970; New York: Grossman, 1973.

Additional Prose: A Bibliography on America, Proprioception, and Other Notes and Essays. Edited by George F. Butterick. Bolinas, CA: Four Seasons, 1974.

The Post Office. Bolinas, CA: Grey Fox, 1975.

The Maximus Poems Volume Three. Edited by Charles Boer and George F. Butterick. New York: Grossman, 1975.

In Adullam's Lair. Provincetown, MA: To the Lighthouse, 1975.

Spearmint & Rosemary. Berkeley: Turtle Island, 1975.

The Horses of the Sea. Santa Barbara: Black Sparrow, 1976.

The Fiery Hunt and Other Plays. Bolinas, CA: Four Seasons, 1977.

Some Early Poems. Iowa City: Windhover, 1978.

Muthologos: The Collected Lectures and Interviews. 2 vols. Edited by George F. Butterick. Bolinas, CA: Four Seasons, 1978–1979.

Charles Olson & Robert Creeley: The Complete Correspondence. Edited by George F. Butterick, later Richard Blevins, vols 1–10. Santa Barbara: Black Sparrow, 1980–1996.

The Maximus Poems. Edited by George F. Butterick. Berkeley: University of California Press, 1983.

The Collected Poems of Charles Olson: Excluding the Maximus Poems. Edited by George F. Butterick. Berkeley: University of California Press, 1987.

A Nation of Nothing but Poetry. Edited by George F. Butterick. Santa Rosa, CA: Black Sparrow, 1989.

In Love, In Sorrow: The Complete Correspondence of Charles Olson and Edward Dahlberg. Edited by Paul Christensen. New York: Paragon House, 1990.

Collected Prose. Edited by Donald Allen and Benjamin Friedlander. Berkeley: University of California Press, 1997.

A Modern Correspondence. With Frances Boldereff. Edited by Ralph Maud and Sharon Thesen. Middletown, CT: Wesleyan University Press, 1999.

Selected Letters. Edited by Ralph Maud. Berkeley: University of California Press, 2000.

Poet to Publisher: Charles Olson's Correspondence with Donald Allen. Edited by Ralph Maud. Vancouver: Talonbooks, 2003.

Muthologos: Lectures and Interviews. Second edition. Edited by Ralph Maud. Vancouver: Talonbooks, 2010.

ANNOTATED INDEX

Index of letters and footnotes. Footnotes abbreviated n.

P

Sharon Thesen, a poet and editor, is professor emerita of Creative Writing at the University of British Columbia, Okanagan. Her research interests include American mid-century and projectivist poetics and the Canadian long poem. She has published nine books of poetry, most recently *Oyama Pink Shale*, *The Good Bacteria*, and *A Pair of Scissors*. She has edited two editions of *The New Long Poem Anthology*, an award-winning selected poems of Phyllis Webb, *The Vision Tree*, and, with Ralph Maud, *Charles Olson and Frances Boldereff: A Modern Correspondence*. She was an editor of the *Capilano Review* when she was teaching English at Capilano College (now University) and continues as one of its contributing editors; at UBC Okanagan she co-edited *Lake: A Journal of Arts and Environment*.

Ralph Maud, a world-renowned expert on the work of Dylan Thomas, Charles Olson, and the ethnography of the Pacific Northwest, is professor emeritus at Simon Fraser University and founder of the Charles Olson Literary Society. He is the author of *Charles Olson Reading*, *Poet to Publisher: Charles Olson's Correspondence with Donald Allen*, and *Charles Olson at the Harbor*, and the editor of *The Selected Letters of Charles Olson* and *Muthologos: Lectures and Interviews*. Maud's work on ethnography includes *Transmission Difficulties: Franz Boas and Tsimshian Mythology*, *The Porcupine Hunter and Other Stories*, and *A Guide to B.C. Indian Myth and Legend*.